HARRAP'S

German phrasebook

Stuart Fortey

Britta Nord

McGraw·Hill

New York   Chicago   San Francisco   Lisbon   London   Madrid   Mexico City
Milan   New Delhi   San Juan   Seoul   Singapore   Sydney   Toronto

ISBN 0-07-146747-5

McGraw-Hill books are available at special quantity discounts to use as
premiums and sales promotions, or for use in corporate training programs.
For more information, please write to the Director of Special Sales,
Professional Publishing, McGraw-Hill, Two Penn Plaza, New York, NY
10121-2298. Or contact your local bookstore.

Reprinted 2006

Editor & Project Manager
Anna Stevenson

Publishing Manager
Patrick White

Prepress
Susan Lawrie

CONTENTS

Introduction	4
Pronunciation	5
Everyday conversation	7
Getting to know people	14
Travelling	22
Accommodation	35
Eating and drinking	43
Food and drink	51
Going out	63
Tourism and sightseeing	70
Sports and games	76
Shopping	83
Photos	91
Banks	94
Post offices	96
Internet cafés and e-mail	99
Telephone	102
Health	107
Problems and emergencies	114
Time and date	118
Numbers	125
English-German dictionary	127
German-English dictionary	154
Grammar	178
Holidays and festivals	185
Useful addresses	188
Conversion tables	191

INTRODUCTION

This brand new English-German phrasebook from Harrap is ideal for anyone wishing to try out their foreign language skills while travelling abroad. The information is practical and clearly presented, helping you to overcome the language barrier and mix with the locals.

Each section features a list of useful words and a selection of common phrases: some of these you will read or hear, while others will help you to express yourself. The simple phonetic transcription system, specifically designed for English speakers, ensures that you will always make yourself understood.

The book also includes a mini bilingual dictionary of around 4,000 words, so that more adventurous users can build on the basic structures and engage in more complex conversations.

Concise information on local culture and customs is provided, along with practical tips to save you time. After all, you're on holiday – time to relax and enjoy yourself! There is also a food and drink glossary to help you make sense of menus, and ensure that you don't miss out on any of the national or regional specialities.

Remember that any effort you make will be appreciated. So don't be shy – have a go!

ABBREVIATIONS USED IN THIS GUIDE

adj	adjective
adv	adverb
f	feminine noun
fpl	feminine plural noun
m	masculine noun
mpl	masculine plural noun
n	noun
pl	plural
prep	preposition
sing	singular
v	verb

PRONUNCIATION

In this book, German words that you might need in order to express yourself are followed by an indication in *italic* of how to pronounce them.

Vowels

The vowel sounds given in *italic* are pronounced as in the following English words:

a	as in	m**a**t	*eu*	as in	chauff**eur**	*oo*	as in	p**oo**l
aa	as in	b**ar**	*ey*	as in	**eye**	*ow*	as in	h**ow**
ay	as in	**way**	*i*	as in	s**i**t	*oy*	as in	b**oy**
e	as in	th**e**	*o*	as in	h**o**t	*u*	as in	p**u**sh
ee	as in	f**ee**	*oh*	see below		*uu*	see below	
eh	as in	g**e**t						

To pronounce the sound *oh*, first of all make the sound *o* and then purse your lips. It is pronounced like the English word "so" but you must keep your lips very rounded and not allow the vowel sound to change halfway through.

To pronounce the sound *uu*, first of all make the sound *ee* and then purse your lips. It is pronounced in almost the same way that the ue in the French word "rue" is pronounced. Sometimes *uu* is pronounced short (as in **müssen** *muu*sen) and sometimes long (as in **süß** *zuus*).

A vowel that is pronounced long (eg **fährt** <u>*fehrt*</u>) is indicated by underlining.

Note that **bold** text indicates that you should stress that syllable.

Consonants

The consonants given in *italic* are pronounced exactly as in English, except for:

ch	as in lo**ch** (not as in **ch**oose)
g	as in **g**uest (not as in **g**inger)
rh	to pronounce this sound, make the *ch* sound (as in lo**ch**) and try to produce an r sound at the same time. The sound *rh* is pronounced in almost the same way that the r in the French word "rue" is pronounced.

Alphabet

The letters of the alphabet are pronounced in German as follows:

a	*aa*	**h**	*haa*	**o**	*oh*	**v**	*fow*
b	*bay*	**i**	*ee*	**p**	*pay*	**w**	*vay*
c	*tsay*	**j**	*yot*	**q**	*koo*	**x**	*iks*
d	*day*	**k**	*kaa*	**r**	*ehrh*	**y**	*uupsilon*
e	*ay*	**l**	*ehl*	**s**	*ehs*	**z**	*tseht*
f	*ehf*	**m**	*ehm*	**t**	*tay*		
g	*gay*	**n**	*ehn*	**u**	*oo*		

EVERYDAY CONVERSATION

Germans tend to greet each other with a handshake. There are two ways to say "you" in German: the familiar **du** (plural form **ihr**) and the formal **Sie**, which is conjugated like the third person plural, ie the same as "they". In professional situations, you should address people as **Herr** (Mr) or **Frau** (Mrs) followed by their surname. Many professionals (teachers, company directors etc) use the title **Doktor**. It is best to address them at first as **Herr/Frau Doktor** followed by their surname. When you are with young people or friends, it is acceptable to use the familiar **du** form – but it is always best to wait until invited to do so. The **Sie** form is given in the following examples as being the one you will need in most situations.

The basics

bye	tschüss *tshuus*
excuse me	entschuldigen Sie *ehntshuldigen zee*
good afternoon	guten Tag *gooten taak*
goodbye	auf Wiedersehen *owf veedezayen*
good evening	guten Abend *gooten aabent*
good morning	guten Morgen *gooten morgen*
goodnight	gute Nacht *goote nacht*
hello	hallo *haloh*
hi	hallo *haloh*
no	nein *neyn*
OK	okay *ohkay*
please	bitte *bite*
sorry	Entschuldigung *ehntshuldigung*
thanks, thank you	danke *danke*
yes	ja *yaa*

Expressing yourself

I'd like ...
ich möchte ...
ish meushte ...

we'd like ...
wir möchten ...
wee-e meushten ...

do you want ...?
möchten Sie ...?
meushten zee ...?

do you have ...?
haben Sie ...?
haaben zee ...?

is there ...?
gibt es ...?
geept ehs ...?

are there any ...?
gibt es ...?
geept ehs ...?

how ...?
wie ...?
vee ...?

why ...?
warum ...?
varhum ...?

when ...?
wann ...?
van ...?

what ...?
was ...?
vas ...?

where is ...?
wo ist ...?
voh ist ...?

where are ...?
wo sind ...?
voh zint ...?

how much is it?
wie viel kostet das?
vee feel kostet das?

what's this?
was ist das?
vas ist das?

do you speak English?
sprechen Sie Englisch?
shprhehshen zee ehnglish?

how are you?
wie geht es Ihnen?
vee gayt ehs eenen?

fine, thanks
danke, gut
danke, goot

thanks very much
vielen Dank
feelen dank

no, thanks
nein, danke
neyn, danke

yes, please
ja, bitte
yaa, bite

where are the toilets, please?
wo ist bitte die Toilette?
voh ist bite dee twalehte?

I'm sorry
es tut mir Leid
ehs toot mee-e leyt

EVERYDAY CONVERSATION

you're welcome	**see you later**
bitte	bis später
bite	*bis shpehte*

Understanding

Achtung	be careful
Ausgang	exit
außer Betrieb	out of order
Eingang	entrance
Eintritt frei	admission free
geöffnet	open
nicht ...	do not ...
Parken verboten	no parking
Rauchen verboten	no smoking
reserviert	reserved
Toiletten	toilets

es gibt ...	**willkommen**
there's/there are ...	welcome

kann ich ...?	**einen Moment bitte**
can I ...?	one moment, please

nehmen Sie doch bitte Platz
please take a seat

macht es Ihnen etwas aus, wenn ...?
do you mind if ...?

PROBLEMS UNDERSTANDING GERMAN

Expressing yourself

pardon?	**what?**
wie bitte?	was?
vee bite?	*vas?*

could you repeat that, please?
könnten Sie das bitte wiederholen?
keunten zee das bite veedehohlen?

could you speak more slowly?
könnten Sie bitte etwas langsamer sprechen?
keunten zee bite ehtvas langsaame shprhehshen?

I don't understand
ich verstehe Sie nicht
ish fehrshtaye zee nisht

I understand a little German
ich verstehe ein bisschen Deutsch
ish fehrshtaye eyn bis-shen doytsh

I hardly speak any German
ich spreche kaum Deutsch
ish shprhehshe kowm doytsh

how do you say … in German?
was heißt … auf Deutsch?
vas heyst … owf doytsh?

how do you spell it?
wie wird das geschrieben?
vee virt das geshrheeben?

what's that called in German?
wie heißt das auf Deutsch?
vee heyst das owf doytsh?

could you write it down for me?
könnten Sie mir das bitte aufschreiben?
keunten zee mee-e das bite owfshrheyben?

I can understand German but I can't speak it
ich verstehe Deutsch, aber ich spreche es nicht
ish fehrshtaye doytsh, aabe ish shprhehshe ehs nisht

Understanding

verstehen Sie Deutsch?
do you understand German?

sprechen Sie Deutsch?
do you speak German?

ich schreibe es Ihnen auf
I'll write it down for you

das heißt …
it means …

SPEAKING ABOUT THE LANGUAGE

Expressing yourself

I've learnt a few words from my phrasebook
ich habe ein paar Wörter aus meinem Sprachführer gelernt
ish haabe eyn paa veurte ows meynem shprhaachfuurhe gelehrnt

I did German at school but I've forgotten everything
ich hatte Deutsch in der Schule, aber ich habe alles vergessen
ish hatte doytsh in daye shoole, aabe ish haabe ales fehrgehsen

I can just about get by
ich kann mich einigermaßen verständlich machen
ish kan mish eynige-maasen fehrshtehntlish machen

I know just a few words
ich kann nur ein oder zwei Wörter
ish kan noo-e eyn ohde tsvey veurte

I find German a difficult language
ich finde, Deutsch ist eine schwierige Sprache
ish finde, doytsh ist eyne shveerhige shprhaache

I know the basics but no more than that
ich weiß nur das Allernötigste
ish veys noo-e das aleneutigste

people speak too quickly for me
die Leute sprechen mir zu schnell
dee loyte shprhehshen mee-e tsoo shnehl

Understanding

Sie haben eine gute Aussprache
you have a good accent

Sie sprechen sehr gut Deutsch
you speak very good German

ASKING THE WAY

Expressing yourself

excuse me, can you tell me where … is, please?
entschuldigen Sie, können Sie mir bitte sagen, wo … ist?
ehntshuldigen zee, keunen zee mee-e bite zaagen, voh … ist?

which way is it to the museum?
wo geht es zum Museum?
voh gayt ehs tsum moozayum?

can you tell me how to get to the railway station?
können Sie mir sagen, wie ich zum Bahnhof komme?
keunen zee mee-e zaagen, vee ish tsum baanhohf kome?

is there ... near here?
gibt es hier in der Nähe ...?
geept ehs hee-e in daye nehe ...?

could you show me on the map?
können Sie mir das auf der Karte zeigen?
keunen zee mee-e das owf daye kaate tseygen?

is there a map of the town somewhere?
gibt es hier irgendwo einen Stadtplan?
geept ehs hee-e irgendvoh eynen shtatplaan?

is it far?	**I'm looking for ...**
ist das weit?	ich suche ...
ist das veyt?	*ish zooche ...*

I'm lost
ich habe mich verlaufen
ish haabe mish fehrlowfen

Understanding

biegen Sie ... ab	turn ...
fahren Sie	go
gehen Sie	go
geradeaus	straight ahead
links	left
rechts	right

sind Sie zu Fuß?	**es ist nicht weit**
are you on foot?	it's not far

mit dem Auto sind es fünf Minuten
it's five minutes away by car

es ist die erste/zweite/dritte Straße links
it's the first/second/third on the left

biegen Sie an der ersten Kreuzung rechts ab
turn right at the first junction

biegen Sie an der Ampel links ab
turn left at the traffic lights

nehmen Sie die nächste Ausfahrt
take the next exit

es sind ungefähr zweihundert Meter
it's about 200 metres

GETTING TO KNOW PEOPLE

The basics

bad	schlecht *shlehsht*
beautiful	schön *sheun*
boring	langweilig *lang*veylish
cheap	billig *bilish*
expensive	teuer *toye*
good	gut *goot*
great	toll *tol*
interesting	interessant *interheh*sant
nice	nett *neht*
not bad	nicht schlecht *nisht shlehsht*
well	gut *goot*
to hate	furchtbar finden *furshtbaa finden*
to like	mögen *meugen*

INTRODUCING YOURSELF AND FINDING OUT ABOUT OTHER PEOPLE

Expressing yourself

my name's ...
ich heiße ...
ish heyse ...

what's your name?
wie heißen Sie?
vee heysen zee?

how do you do?
wie geht's?
vee gayts?

pleased to meet you!
angenehm!
angenaym!

this is my husband/my wife
das ist mein Mann/meine Frau
das ist meyn man/meyne frhow

this is my partner, Karen
das ist meine Lebensgefährtin Karen
*das ist meyne lay*bensge<u>feh</u>rtin karen

I'm from …
ich komme aus …
ish kome ows …

where are you from?
woher kommen Sie?
voh-haye komen zee?

how old are you?
wie alt bist du?
vee alt bist doo?

I'm 22
ich bin zweiundzwanzig
ish bin tsvey-unt-tsvan-tsish

what do you do for a living?
was machen Sie?
vas machen zee?

are you a student?
studieren Sie?
shtoodeerhen zee?

I work
ich arbeite
ish aabeyte

I'm studying law
ich studiere Jura
ish shtoodeerhe yoorha

I'm a teacher
ich bin Lehrer/Lehrerin
ish bin layrhe/layrherhin

I stay at home with the children
ich bin Hausmann/Hausfrau
ish bin howsman/howsfrhow

I work part-time
ich habe eine Teilzeitstelle
ish haabe eyne teyl-tseyt-shtehle

I work in marketing
ich arbeite im Marketingbereich
ish aabeyte im marketingberheysh

I'm retired
ich bin Rentner/Rentnerin
ish bin rhehntne/rhehntnerhin

I'm self-employed
ich bin selbstständig
ish bin zehlpst-shtehndish

we're Welsh
wir sind aus Wales
vee-e zint ows wayls

I have two children
ich habe zwei Kinder
ish haabe tsvey kinde

we don't have any children
wir haben keine Kinder
vee-e haaben keyne kinde

two boys and a girl
zwei Jungen und ein Mädchen
tsvey yungen unt eyn mehtshen

the boy is five, the girl is two
der Junge ist fünf, das Mädchen zwei
daye yunge ist fuunf, das mehtshen tsvey

I'm English
ich bin Engländer/Engländerin
ish bin ehnglehnde/ehnglehnderhin

have you ever been to Britain?
waren Sie schon einmal in Großbritannien?
vaarhen zee shohn eynmaal in grhohs-brhitanien?

Understanding

sind Sie Engländer/Engländerin?
are you English?

ich kenne England ganz gut
I know England quite well

wir machen auch Urlaub hier
we're on holiday here too

ich würde gerne einmal nach Schottland fahren
I'd love to go to Scotland one day

TALKING ABOUT YOUR STAY

Expressing yourself

I'm here on business
ich bin geschäftlich hier
ish bin geshehftlish hee-e

we're on holiday
wir machen Urlaub
vee-e machen oo-e-lowp

I arrived three days ago
ich bin vor drei Tagen angekommen
ish bin fohe drhey taagen angekomen

we've been here for a week
wir sind seit einer Woche hier
vee-e zint zeyt eyne voche hee-e

we're just passing through
wir sind nur auf der Durchreise
vee-e zint noo-e owf daye dursh-rheyze

I'm only here for a long weekend
ich bin nur für ein langes Wochenende hier
ish bin noo-e fuu-e eyn langes vochen-ehnde hee-e

this is our first time in Germany
wir sind zum ersten Mal in Deutschland
vee-e zint tsum ayesten maal in doytshlant

we're here to celebrate our wedding anniversary
wir feiern hier unseren Hochzeitstag
vee-e feyern hee-e unzerhen hoch-tseyts-taak

we're on our honeymoon
wir sind auf Hochzeitsreise
vee-e zint owf hoch-tseyts-rheyze

we're here with friends
wir sind mit Freunden hier
vee-e zint mit froynden hee-e

we're touring around
wir machen eine Rundreise
vee-e machen eyne rhunt-rheyze

we managed to get a cheap flight
wir haben einen billigen Flug bekommen
vee-e haaben eynen biligen flook bekomen

we're thinking about buying a house here
wir überlegen, hier ein Haus zu kaufen
vee-e uube-laygen, hee-e eyn hows tsoo kowfen

Understanding

viel Spaß!
have a good time!

einen schönen Urlaub noch!
enjoy the rest of your holiday!

wie lange bleiben Sie?
how long are you staying?

gefällt es Ihnen hier?
do you like it here?

sind Sie zum ersten Mal in Deutschland?
is this your first time in Germany?

waren Sie schon im Schwarzwald?
have you been to the Black Forest?

STAYING IN TOUCH

Expressing yourself

we should stay in touch
wir sollten in Kontakt bleiben
vee-e zolten in kontakt bleyben

I'll give you my e-mail address
ich gebe Ihnen meine E-Mail-Adresse
ish gaybe eenen meyne eemayl-adrhehse

here's my address, if ever you come to England/Scotland
hier ist meine Adresse, falls Sie einmal nach England/Schottland kommen sollten
hee-e ist meyne adrhehse, fals zee eynmaal nach ehnglant/shotlant komen zolten

Understanding

würden Sie mir Ihre Adresse geben?
will you give me your address?

haben Sie eine E-Mail-Adresse?
do you have an e-mail address?

Sie sind bei uns jederzeit willkommen
you're always welcome to come and stay with us

EXPRESSING YOUR OPINION

> **Some informal expressions**
>
> **es war spitze** it was great
> **wir haben uns köstlich amüsiert** we had a great time
> **es war ein Reinfall** it was a disaster

Expressing yourself

I really like the hotel
das Hotel gefällt mir wirklich gut
das hohtehl gefehlt mee-e virklish goot

I don't like our neighbours
ich mag die Nachbarn nicht
ish maag dee nachbaan nisht

I didn't like the trip to ...
der Ausflug nach ... hat mir nicht gefallen
daye owsflook nach ... hat mee-e nisht gefalen

I loved the museum
das Museum hat mir sehr gut gefallen
das moozayum haat mee-e zaye goot gefalen

I really liked the people
ich fand die Leute wirklich nett
ish fant dee loyte virklish neht

I love this place
ich finde es sehr schön hier
ish finde ehs zaye sheun hee-e

I would like to come back
ich würde gerne wieder kommen
ish vuurde gehrne veede komen

I would have liked to stay longer
ich wäre gerne länger geblieben
ish wehre gehrne lehnge gebleeben

I find it …
ich finde es …
ish finde ehs …

I found it …
ich fand es …
ish fant ehs …

it's lovely
es ist herrlich
ehs ist hehrlish

it was lovely
es war herrlich
ehs vaa hehrlish

I agree
das finde ich auch
das finde ish owch

I don't agree
das finde ich nicht
das finde ish nisht

I don't know
ich weiß nicht
ish veys nisht

I don't mind
es ist mir egal
ehs ist mee-e ehgaal

I don't like the sound of it
das klingt nicht gut
das klingt nisht goot

it sounds interesting
das klingt interessant
das klingt interhehsant

it really annoys me
ich finde es wirklich langweilig
ish finde ehs virklish langveylish

it was boring
es war langweilig
ehs vaa langveylish

it's a rip-off
das ist der reinste Nepp
das ist daye rheynste nehp

it gets very busy at night
hier ist abends sehr viel los
hee-e ist aabents zaye feel lohs

it's too busy
es ist zu viel los
ehs ist tsoo feel lohs

it's very quiet
es ist sehr ruhig
ehs ist zaye rhooish

I really enjoyed myself
es hat mir wirklich gefallen
ehs hat mee-e virklish gefalen

we had a great time
es hat uns viel Spaß gemacht
ehs hat uns feel shpaas gemacht

we felt very much at home
wir haben uns sehr wohl gefühlt
vee-e haaben uns zaye vohl gefuult

we found a great hotel
wir hatten ein tolles Hotel
vee-e haten eyn toles hohtehl

there was a really good atmosphere
die Atmosphäre war wirklich gut
dee atmohsfehrhe vaa virklish goot

we met some nice people
wir haben nette Leute kennen gelernt
vee-e haaben nehte loyte kehnen gelehrnt

Understanding

gefällt Ihnen ...?
do you like ...?

ich empfehle ...
I recommend ...

es ist nicht allzu überlaufen
there aren't too many tourists

am Wochenende ist dort zu viel los
at the weekend it's too busy

es ist nicht so toll wie behauptet wird
it's a bit overrated

hat es Ihnen gefallen?
did you enjoy yourself/yourselves?

es ist eine herrliche Gegend
it's a lovely area

TALKING ABOUT THE WEATHER

> **Some informal expressions**
>
> **es regnet in Strömen** it's pouring with rain
> **die Sonne brennt** the sun's blazing
> **es herrschte eine Affenhitze** it was boiling hot

Expressing yourself

have you seen the weather forecast for tomorrow?
wissen Sie, wie morgen das Wetter werden soll?
visen zee, vee morgen das vehte wayeden zol?

it's going to be nice
es wird schön
ehs virt sheun

it isn't going to be nice
es wird nicht schön
ehs virt nisht sheun

it's really hot
es ist sehr heiß
ehs ist zaye heys

it gets cold at night
nachts wird es kalt
nachts virt ehs kalt

it's thirty in the shade/minus ten
es sind dreißig Grad im Schatten/minus zehn Grad
ehs zint drhey-sish grhaat im shaten/meenus tsayn grhaat

the weather was beautiful
es war wunderschönes Wetter
ehs vaa vunde-sheunes vehte

it rained a few times
es hat ein paar Mal geregnet
ehs hat eyn paa maal gerhaygnet

there was a thunderstorm
es hat ein Gewitter gegeben
ehs hat eyn gevite gegayben

it's very humid here
es ist sehr feucht hier
ehs ist zaye foysht hee-e

it's been lovely all week
es war die ganze Woche herrliches Wetter
ehs vaa dee gantse voche hehrlishes vehte

we've been lucky with the weather
wir hatten Glück mit dem Wetter
vee-e haten gluuk mit daym vehte

Understanding

es soll regnen
it's supposed to rain

morgen wird es wieder heiß
it will be hot again tomorrow

nächste Woche soll es schön werden
they've forecast good weather for next week

TRAVELLING

The basics

airport	der Flughafen *daye floog*haafen
boarding	das Boarding *das bor*ding
boarding card	die Bordkarte *dee bord*kaate
boat	das Schiff *das shif*
bus	der Bus *daye bus*
bus station	der Busbahnhof *daye bus*baanhof
bus stop	die Bushaltestelle *dee bus*halte-shtehle
car	das Auto *das ow*toh
check-in	der Check-in *daye tshehk-*in
coach	der Bus *daye bus*
ferry	die Fähre *dee feh*rhe
flight	der Flug *daye flook*
gate	das Gate *das gayt*
left-luggage (office)	die Gepäckaufbewahrung *dee ge*pehk-owfbevaarhung
luggage	das Gepäck *das ge*pehk
map	(of area) die Karte *dee kaa*te; (of town) der Stadtplan *daye shtat*plaan
motorway	die Autobahn *dee ow*tohbaan
passport	der Pass *daye pas*
plane	das Flugzeug *das floog*tsoyk
platform	das Gleis *das gleys*
railway station	der Bahnhof *daye baan*hof
return (ticket)	die Rückfahrkarte *dee rhuuk*faarkaate
road	die Straße *dee shtrhaa*se
shuttle bus	der Shuttle *daye sha*tel
single (ticket)	die einfache Fahrkarte *dee eyn*fache *faar*kaate
street	die Straße *dee shtrhaa*se
streetmap	der Stadtplan *daye shtat*plaan
taxi	das Taxi *das tak*si
terminal	das Terminal *das teur*minel
ticket	(for train, coach, bus, boat) die Fahrkarte *dee faar*kaate; (for plane) das Flugticket *das floog*tiket
timetable	der Fahrplan *daye faar*plaan

town centre	das Stadtzentrum *das stat-tsehntrum*
train	der Zug *daye tsook*
tram	die Straßenbahn *dee shtraasenbaan*
underground	die U-Bahn *die oobaan*
underground station	die U-Bahn-Station *dee oobaan-shtatsiohn*
to hire	mieten *meeten*
to reserve	reservieren *rhehzehrveerhen*

Expressing yourself

where can I buy tickets?
wo kann ich Fahrkarten kaufen?
voh kan ish faarkaaten kowfen?

(a single to) Hamburg/the town centre/the airport, please
(eine Fahrkarte) nach Hamburg/ins Stadtzentrum/zum Flughafen bitte
(eyne faarkaate) nach Hamburg/ins stat-tsehntrhum/tsum flooghaafen bite

a return to Cologne, please
eine Rückfahrkarte nach Köln bitte
eyne rhuukfaarkaate nach keuln bite

I'd like to reserve a seat
ich möchte eine Platzreservierung
ish meushte eyne plats-rhehzehrveerhung

how much is a ticket to Heidelberg/the castle?
wie viel kostet eine Fahrkarte nach Heidelberg/zum Schloss?
vee feel kostet eyne faarkaate nach Heydelbehrg/tsum shlos?

are there any concessions for students?
gibt es eine Ermäßigung für Studenten?
geept ehs eyne ehrmehsigung fuu-e shtoodehnten?

could I have a timetable, please?
könnte ich bitte einen Fahrplan haben?
keunte ish bite eynen faarplaan haaben?

is there an earlier/later train/coach?
gibt es einen früheren/späteren Zug/Bus?
geept ehs eynen frhuuerhen/spehterhen tsook/bus?

how long does the journey/the flight take?
wie lange dauert die Fahrt/der Flug?
vee lange dowert dee faart/daye flook?

is this seat free?
ist hier noch frei?
ist hee-e noch frhey?

I'm sorry, there's someone sitting there
es tut mir Leid, hier sitzt schon jemand
ehs toot mee-e leyt, hee-e zitst shohn yaymant

Understanding

Making sense of abbreviations
Nowadays many signs use pictorial symbols, but here are some abbreviations you may find on timetables, on arrivals and departures boards and on tickets:

BC = BahnCard	card allowing reduced-price rail travel
Bf = Bahnhof	station
Di = Dienstag	Tuesday
Do = Donnerstag	Thursday
erw. = erwartet	expected *(plane)*
Fr = Freitag	Friday
H = Hinfahrt	outward journey
Hbf = Hauptbahnhof	main station
Kl = Klasse	class
Mi = Mittwoch	Wednesday
Mo = Montag	Monday
plan = planmäßig	scheduled *(plane)*
R = Rückfahrt	return journey
Sa = Samstag	Saturday
So = Sonntag	Sunday
Term. = Terminal	terminal
Umst. = Umsteigen	change

Abfahrt/Abflug	departures
Ankunft	arrivals

annulliert	cancelled *(plane)*
Ausgang	exit
Auskunft	information
Betreten verboten	no entry
Damen	ladies *(toilet)*
Eingang	entrance
Fahrscheine	tickets
fällt aus	cancelled *(train)*
Herren	gents *(toilet)*
Toiletten	toilets
Verbindungen	connections
Verspätung	delay

es ist alles ausgebucht
everything is fully booked

BY PLANE

There are many domestic flights available. Besides Lufthansa (the national carrier), there are various smaller airlines which link the main cities. They also fly to smaller airports and the North Frisian Islands. The main airports are at Frankfurt, Munich, Berlin, Düsseldorf, Dresden, Hanover, Stuttgart and Nuremberg. Airports can be reached by **U-Bahn** (underground) or **S-Bahn** (suburban rail network) from the city centres, or by coach from other towns and cities.

Expressing yourself

where's the British Airways check-in?
wo ist der Check-in von British Airways?
*voh ist daye **tshehk**-in fon British Airways?*

I've got an e-ticket
ich habe ein Online-Ticket
*ish **haabe** eyn **on**leyn-tiket*

what time do we board?
wann beginnt das Boarding?
*van be**gint** das **bor**ding?*

one suitcase and one piece of hand luggage
ein Koffer und ein Handgepäckstück
eyn kofe unt eyn hantgepehk-shtuuk

I'd like to confirm my return flight
ich möchte meinen Rückflug bestätigen
ish meushte meynen rhuukflook beshtehtigen

one of my suitcases is missing
einer meiner Koffer fehlt
eyne meyne kofe faylt

my luggage hasn't arrived
mein Gepäck ist nicht angekommen
meyn gepehk ist nisht angekomen

the plane was two hours late
das Flugzeug hatte zwei Stunden Verspätung
das floogtsoyk hate tsvey shtunden fehrshpehtung

I've missed my connection
ich habe meinen Anschluss verpasst
ish haabe meynen anshlus fehrpast

I've left something on the plane
ich habe etwas im Flugzeug vergessen
ish haabe ehtvas im floogtsoyk fehrgehsen

I want to report the loss of my luggage
ich möchte den Verlust meines Gepäcks melden
ish meushte dayn fehrlust meynes gepehks mehlden

Understanding

Abflughalle	departure lounge
anmeldefreie Waren	nothing to declare
anmeldepflichtige Waren	goods to declare
aufgerufen	now boarding
erwartet	expected
Gepäckausgabe	baggage reclaim
Gepäckkontrolle	baggage control
Inlandsflüge	domestic flights
Passkontrolle	passport control

planmäßig   scheduled
zollfrei   duty-free
Zollkontrolle   customs

bitte warten Sie in der Abflughalle
please wait in the departure lounge

möchten Sie einen Fensterplatz oder einen Platz am Gang?
would you like a window seat or an aisle seat?

Sie müssen in ... umsteigen
you'll have to change at …

wie viele Gepäckstücke haben Sie?
how many pieces of luggage do you have?

haben Sie Ihr Gepäck selbst gepackt?
did you pack all your luggage yourself?

hat Ihnen jemand etwas mitgegeben?
has anyone given you anything to take on board?

Ihr Gepäck hat fünf Kilo Übergewicht
your luggage is five kilos overweight

hier ist Ihre Bordkarte   **das Boarding beginnt um ...**
here's your boarding card   boarding will begin at …

bitte begeben Sie sich zu Gate Nummer ...
please proceed to gate number …

dies ist der letzte Aufruf für ...
this is a final call for …

der Flug ... ist bereit zum Einsteigen
flight … is ready for boarding

BY TRAIN, COACH, BUS, UNDERGROUND, TRAM

Germany has an excellent rail network, particularly since the introduction of the **ICE** high-speed trains. However, journeys in the former East Germany can still be rather slow. Prices are quite high, but **DB** (**Deutsche Bahn**, the national rail company) offers various discounts (**BahnCard**, **Sparpreis** and reduced-price tickets for people under 26): ask at the booking office for more information. On some trains, reservations are compulsory; these are marked with a circled **R** on timetables.

Big cities like Berlin, Hanover, Munich and Frankfurt have underground systems (**U-Bahn**). The **S-Bahn** is the network serving the suburbs. You can buy **Tageskarten** (day tickets), **Wochenkarten** (weekly season tickets) or **Mehrfahrtenkarten** (multi-journey tickets), all of which are valid for the entire urban network (including the **S-Bahn**).

Bus and tram tickets can be bought from machines at stops or in stations. You can also buy a single ticket (**Einzelfahrschein**) from the driver, but if you intend to make several journeys this works out more expensive than buying a day ticket, a weekly season ticket or a multi-journey ticket. Stops are clearly signalled on all forms of transport, usually by means of an announcement and sometimes also an electronic sign.

Coaches provide links to towns that are not served by a railway station. They are also used for excursions and for getting to airports in nearby cities.

Expressing yourself

can I have a map of the underground, please?
könnte ich bitte eine U-Bahn-Karte haben?
keunte ish bite eyne oobaankaate haaben?

what time is the next train to …?
wann fährt der nächste Zug nach …?
van fehrt daye nehkste tsook nach …?

what time is the last train?
wann fährt der letzte Zug?
van fehrt daye lehtste tsook?

where can I catch a bus to …?
wo fährt der Bus nach … ab?
voh fehrt daye bus nach … ap?

which platform is it for …?
an welchem Gleis fährt der Zug nach …?
an vehlshem gleys fehrt daye tsook nach …?

which line do I take to get to …?
welche Linie fährt nach …?
vehlshe leenie fehrt nach …?

is this the stop for …?
ist dies die Haltestelle für …?
ist dees dee halte-shtehle fuu-e …?

I've missed my train/bus
ich habe den Zug/Bus verpasst
ish haabe dayn tsook/bus fehrpast

is this where the coach leaves for the airport?
fährt hier der Bus zum Flughafen ab?
fehrt hee-e daye bus tsum flooghaafen ap?

can you tell me when I need to get off?
können Sie mir bitte sagen, wann ich aussteigen muss?
keunen zee mee-e bite zaagen, van ish ows-shteygen mus?

Understanding

ab	departs
an	arrives
Fahrtziele	destinations
nächster Halt	next stop
Reisezentrum	ticket office
Reservierungen	reservations
Sofortfahrer	tickets for travel today
Tageskarte	day ticket
Wochenkarte	weekly season ticket
zu den Zügen	to the trains

ein Stück weiter auf der rechten Seite ist eine Haltestelle
there's a stop a bit further along on the right

passend zahlen
no change given

der Zug hält in …
this train calls at …

Sie müssen in ... umsteigen
you'll have to change at ...

Sie müssen den Bus Nummer ... nehmen
you need to get the number ... bus

BY CAR

The speed limit is 50 kph in built-up areas and 100 kph on A-roads. There is no speed limit on motorways (**Autobahnen**). Be careful with motorway exits: there is often little prior warning and they can be badly lit at night. Motorways are toll-free and are indicated by a large A on a blue sign. By law seatbelts must be worn in the front and back. Cars run on lead-free petrol (**bleifreies Benzin**), and four-star is no longer available. When driving in town, remember to overtake trams on the right and never overtake them at stops. Many city centres are pedestrianized with no entry for cars. In towns and cities you will find parking places where you can park free for the period indicated as long as you use a parking disc (**Parkscheibe**) which you set to the time you arrive and leave in your car. In a multi-storey car park (**Parkhaus**) there are often special parking places, close to the exit, for women who are driving on their own; these are indicated by the word **Frauenparkplatz**. Should you break down, you can call **ADAC**, a breakdown service which operates in all cities (tel: 0180 2222 222, drop the first 0 if calling from a mobile). You will be charged, but you may be able to claim some of this back later from your own breakdown service, as long as you have the correct European cover.

Hitchhiking (which is forbidden on motorways) is not common practice in Germany. Instead, for a small fee a **Mitfahrzentrale** (car-sharing agency), which you will find in all large towns, will put you in touch with a driver (who will charge about half as much as the same journey would cost by train). This can also be done over the Internet; in this case there is no agency fee and you contact the driver directly by e-mail.

Expressing yourself

where can I find a petrol station?
wo ist die nächste Tankstelle?
voh ist dee nehkste tankshtehle?

is the petrol station open at night as well?
ist die Tankstelle nachts geöffnet?
ist dee tankshtehle nachts ge-eufnet?

(pump) number ... please
Nummer ...
nume ...

we got stuck in a traffic jam
wir standen im Stau
vee-e shtanden im shtow

the battery's dead
die Batterie ist leer
dee baterhee ist laye

I've broken down
mein Auto ist stehen geblieben
meyn owtoh ist shtayen gebleeben

we've run out of petrol
der Tank ist leer
daye tank ist laye

we've just had an accident
wir hatten gerade einen Unfall
vee-e haten gerhaade eynen unfal

is there a garage near here?
ist hier in der Nähe eine Werkstatt?
ist hee-e in daye nehe eyne vehrkshtat?

can you help us to push the car?
können Sie uns helfen, das Auto anzuschieben?
keunen zee uns hehlfen, das owtoh an-tsoo-sheeben?

I've got a puncture and my spare tyre is flat
ich habe eine Reifenpanne und mein Reservereifen ist platt
ish haabe eyne rheyfenpane unt meyn rhehzehrve-rheyfen ist plat

I've lost my car keys
ich habe meinen Autoschlüssel verloren
ish haabe meynen owtoh-shluusel fehrlohrhen

how long will it take to repair?
wie lange dauert die Reparatur?
vee lange dowert dee rhehparhatoo-e?

Hiring a car

I'd like to hire a car for a week
ich möchte für eine Woche ein Auto mieten
ish meushte fuu-e eyne voche eyn owtoh meeten

an automatic (car)
ein Auto mit Automatik
eyn owtoh mit owtohmaatik

I'd like to take out comprehensive insurance
ich möchte eine Vollkaskoversicherung abschließen
ish meushte eyne folkaskoh-fehrzisherhung apshleesen

Getting a taxi

is there a taxi rank near here?
ist hier in der Nähe ein Taxistand?
ist hee-e in daye nehe eyn taksi-shtant?

I'd like to go to Neuhausen/the railway station
ich möchte nach Neuhausen/zum Bahnhof
ish meushte nach noyhowzen/tsum baanhohf

I'd like to book a taxi for 8pm
ich möchte ein Taxi für 20 Uhr bestellen
ish meushte eyn taksi fuur tsvan-tsish oo-e beshtehlen

you can drop me off here, thanks
Sie können hier anhalten
zee keunen hee-e anhalten

how much will it be to go to the airport?
wie viel kostet die Fahrt zum Flughafen?
vee feel kostet dee faart tsum flooghaafen?

Hitchhiking

could you take me as far as …?
können Sie mich bis … mitnehmen?
keunen zee mish bis … mitnaymen?

I'm going to …
ich will nach …
ish vil nach …

can you drop me off here?
können Sie mich hier absetzen?
keunen zee mish hee-e apzehtsen?

thanks for the lift
danke fürs Mitnehmen
danke fuu-es mitnaymen

we hitched a lift
wir sind getrampt
vee-e zint getrhampt

Understanding

alle Richtungen	all directions
andere Richtungen	other directions
Ausfahrt	exit
Autovermietung	car hire
besetzt	full *(car park)*
Bitte einordnen	get in lane
Einfahrt	entrance
frei	spaces *(in car park)*
langsam	slow
Motor abstellen	switch off your engine
Parken verboten	no parking
Parkhaus	multi-storey car park
Parkplatz	car park
Parkschein aufbewahren	keep your ticket

ich brauche Ihren Führerschein, einen Ausweis und Ihre Kreditkarte
I'll need your driving licence, another form of ID and your credit card

Sie müssen eine Kaution in Höhe von 150 Euro zahlen
there's a 150-euro deposit to pay

in Ordnung, steigen Sie ein, ich nehme Sie bis … mit
all right, get in, I'll take you as far as …

BY BOAT

The main ferry services to Scandinavia depart from Kiel and Travemünde in Schleswig-Holstein, and Rostock and Sassnitz in Mecklenburg-West Pomerania. Services to the UK depart from Hamburg. Fares and timetables vary according to the season.

From April to October, boat trips and cruises on the many lakes and rivers are an excellent way to see the country. There are frequent departures to the North Frisian Islands, as well as trips down the Rhine and cruises on the Moselle and Elbe. In summer, you can go sailing on Lake Constance (**Bodensee**). Hamburg offers boat trips around the harbour, while in Berlin the cruise between the capital and Potsdam (**Wannsee**) is very popular.

Expressing yourself

how long is the crossing?	**I'm feeling seasick**
wie lange dauert die Überfahrt?	mir ist schlecht
*vee lange dowert dee **uu**befaart?*	*mee-e ist shlesht*

Understanding

nächste Überfahrt um ...	next crossing at ...
Passagiere ohne Fahrzeug	foot passengers
Rundfahrt	cruise

Hotel rates do not vary much, if at all, according to the season. It is best to book ahead, particularly in summer. Prices are higher in big cities such as Berlin, Frankfurt, Hamburg and Munich, and there is no longer any price difference between the east of the country and the west. The quality of hotels is generally very good, so there is little to gain by staying in a luxury hotel (unless you are keen to have additional facilities such as a gym or sauna). The German National Tourist Board (see the Useful Addresses chapter) has lists of hotels to suit all budgets.

Large towns have a good selection of bed and breakfasts (**Pensionen**), though there are fewer of them in villages. These are family-run places with a limited number of rooms, and are comfortable even if not luxurious. Breakfast is included and sometimes lunch and dinner are provided too. Look out for a sign in the window saying **Zimmer frei** (vacancies).

Campsites in Germany are well equipped. Note that you may have to pay for showers, hot water and even toilet paper. The German National Tourist Board (see the Useful Addresses chapter) provides information about camping and caravanning.

There are about 600 youth hostels (**Jugendherbergen**) in Germany. Membership of the International Youth Hostel Federation is accepted throughout the country, but even if you are not a member you can stay in a hostel upon payment of an extra charge. Hostels have single, double and multi-occupancy rooms. Bed linen is provided. You can get more information from the German Youth Hostel Association (DJH) – see the Useful Addresses chapter.

The basics

bath	die Badewanne *dee baadevane*
bathroom	das Bad *das baat*
bathroom with shower	das Bad mit Dusche *das baat mit dooshe*

bed	das Bett *das beht*
bed and breakfast	die Pension *dee pehnziohn*
cable television	das Kabelfernsehen *das kaabelfehrnzayen*
campsite	der Campingplatz *daye kehmpingplats*
caravan	der Wohnwagen *daye vohnvaagen*
cottage	das Ferienhaus *das fayrhienhows*
double bed	das Doppelbett *das dopel-beht*
double room	das Doppelzimmer *das dopel-tsime*
family room	das Mehrbettzimmer *das mayebeht-tsime*
flat	die Wohnung *dee vohnung*
full board	die Vollpension *dee folpehnziohn*
half-board	die Halbpension *dee halp-pehnziohn*
hotel	das Hotel *das hohtehl*
key	der Schlüssel *daye shluusel*
rent	die Miete *dee meete*
room with en-suite bathroom	das Zimmer mit eigenem Bad *das tsime mit eygenem baat*
self-catering accommodation	(flat) die Ferienwohnung *dee fayrhienvohnung*; (house) das Ferienhaus *das fayrhienhows*
shower	die Dusche *dee dooshe*
single bed	das Einzelbett *das eyntsel-beht*
single room	das Einzelzimmer *das eyntsel-tsime*
tenant	der Mieter *daye meete*
tent	das Zelt *das tsehlt*
toilets	die Toiletten *dee twalehten*
youth hostel	die Jugendherberge *dee yoogent-hehrbehrge*
to book	buchen *boochen*
to rent	mieten *meeten*
to reserve	reservieren *rehzehrveerhen*

Expressing yourself

I have a reservation
ich habe reserviert
ish haabe rhehzehrveert

the name's ...	do you take credit cards?
mein Name ist ...	kann ich mit Kreditkarte bezahlen?
meyn naame ist ...	*kan ish mit krhehdeetkaate betsaalen?*

Understanding

ausgebucht	full
Privat	private
Rezeption	reception
Toiletten	toilets
Zimmer frei	vacancies

ich bräuchte bitte Ihren Ausweis
could I see your passport, please?

füllen Sie bitte dieses Formular aus
could you fill in this form, please?

HOTELS

Expressing yourself

do you have any vacancies?	for three nights
haben Sie noch Zimmer frei?	für drei Nächte
haaben zee noch tsime frhey?	*fuu-e drhey nehshte*

how much is a double room per night?
wie viel kostet ein Doppelzimmer für eine Nacht?
vee feel kostet eyn dopeltsime fuu-e eyne nacht?

I'd like to reserve a double room/a single room
ich möchte ein Doppelzimmer/ein Einzelzimmer reservieren
ish meushte eyn dopel-tsime/eyn eyntsel-tsime rhehzehrveerhen

would it be possible to stay an extra night?
kann ich noch eine Nacht länger bleiben?
kan ish noch eyne nacht lehnge bleyben?

do you have any rooms available for tonight?
haben Sie für heute Nacht noch Zimmer frei?
haaben zee fuu-e hoyte nacht noch tsime frhey?

do you have any family rooms?
haben Sie Mehrbettzimmer?
haaben zee maybeht-tsime?

would it be possible to add an extra bed?
können Sie ein zusätzliches Bett in das Zimmer stellen?
keunen zee eyn tsoozehtslishes beht in das tsime shtehlen?

could I see the room first?
könnte ich das Zimmer bitte erst sehen?
keunte ish das tsime bite ayest zayen?

do you have anything bigger/quieter?
haben Sie ein größeres/ruhigeres Zimmer?
haaben zee eyn greuserhes/rhooigerhes tsime?

that's fine, I'll take it
in Ordnung, ich nehme es
in ordnung, ish nayme ehs

is breakfast included?
ist das Frühstück inbegriffen?
ist das frhuustuuk inbegrhifen?

could you recommend any other hotels?
können Sie mir ein anderes Hotel empfehlen?
keunen zee mee-e eyn anderhes hohtehl ehmpfaylen?

what time do you serve breakfast?
wann gibt es Frühstück?
van geept ehs frhuustuuk?

is there a lift?
gibt es einen Aufzug?
geept ehs eynen owftsook?

the air conditioning isn't working
die Klimaanlage funktioniert nicht
dee kleema-anlaage funktsiohneert nisht

is the hotel near the centre of town?
ist das Hotel in der Nähe des Stadtzentrums?
ist das hohtehl in daye nehe dehs stat-tsehntrums?

what time will the room be ready?
wann ist das Zimmer fertig?
van ist das tsime fehrtish?

the key for room ..., please
den Schlüssel für Zimmer Nummer ... bitte
dayn shluusel fuu-e tsime nume ... bite

could I have an extra blanket?
könnte ich bitte noch eine Decke haben?
*keun*te ish *bite* noch *eyne* dehke *haa*ben?

Understanding

tut mir Leid, wir sind ausgebucht
I'm sorry, but we're full

wir haben nur ein Einzelzimmer
we only have a single room available

für wie viele Nächte?
how many nights is it for?

wie ist Ihr Name?
what's your name, please?

Check-in ist ab 12 Uhr
check-in is from midday

Check-out ist um 11 Uhr
you have to check out before 11am

Frühstück gibt es zwischen 7.30 und 9.00 Uhr im Restaurant
breakfast is served in the restaurant between 7:30 and 9:00

Ihr Zimmer ist noch nicht fertig
your room isn't ready yet

Sie können Ihr Gepäck hier lassen
you can leave your bags here

YOUTH HOSTELS

Expressing yourself

do you have space for two people for tonight?
haben Sie für heute Nacht noch zwei Betten frei?
*haa*ben zee *fuu*-e *hoy*te nacht noch tsvey *behten frhey?*

we've booked two beds for three nights
wir haben zwei Betten für drei Nächte reserviert
*vee-e haa*ben tsvey *beh*ten *fuu*-e drhey *nehsh*te rhehzehr*veert*

could I leave my backpack here?
kann ich meinen Rucksack hier lassen?
*kan ish **mey**nen **rhuk**zak hee-e **las**en?*

I'll come back for it around 7 o'clock
ich hole ihn gegen 7 Uhr ab
*ish **hoh**le een **gay**gen **zee**ben oo-e ap*

do you have somewhere we could leave our bikes?
können wir unsere Räder irgendwo unterstellen?
*keunen vee-e **un**zere **reh**de **irgent**voh unte-shtehlen?*

there's no hot water
es kommt kein heißes Wasser
*ehs komt keyn **hey**ses **va**se*

the sink's blocked
das Waschbecken ist verstopft
*das **vash**behken ist fehr**shtopft***

Understanding

haben Sie einen Jugendherbergsausweis?
do you have a membership card?

Bettwäsche wird gestellt
bed linen is provided

die Jugendherberge ist bis 18 Uhr geschlossen
the hostel reopens at 6pm

SELF-CATERING

Expressing yourself

we're looking for somewhere to rent near a town
wir möchten etwas in der Nähe einer Stadt mieten
*vee-e **meush**ten **eht**vas in daye **neh**e eyne shtat **mee**ten*

where do we pick up/leave the keys?
wo sollen wir den Schlüssel abholen/abgeben?
*voh **zol**en vee-e dayn **shluus**el **ap**hohlen/**ap**gayben?*

is electricity included in the price?
ist der Strom im Preis inbegriffen?
ist daye shtrohm im preys inbegrhifen?

are bed linen and towels provided?
werden Bettwäsche und Handtücher gestellt?
vehrden behtwehshe unt hant-tuushe geshtehlt?

is a car necessary?
braucht man ein Auto?
brhowcht man eyn owtoh?

is there a garden?
gibt es einen Garten?
geept ehs eynen gaaten?

is the accommodation suitable for elderly people?
ist die Wohnung/das Haus für ältere Leute geeignet?
ist dee vohnung/das hows fuu-e ehltere loyte ge-eygnet?

where is the nearest supermarket?
wo ist der nächste Supermarkt?
voh ist daye nehkste zoopemaakt?

Understanding

bitte hinterlassen Sie das Haus in sauberem und ordentlichem Zustand
please leave the house clean and tidy when you go

das Haus ist voll eingerichtet
the house is fully furnished

im Preis ist alles inbegriffen
everything is included in the price

in dieser Gegend braucht man unbedingt ein Auto
you really do need a car in this part of the country

CAMPING

Expressing yourself

is there a campsite near here?
gibt es hier in der Nähe einen Campingplatz?
geept ehs hee-e in daye nehe eynen kehmpingplats?

I'd like to book a space for a two-person tent for three nights
ich möchte einen Zeltplatz für zwei Personen und drei Nächte buchen
ish **meush**te **ey**nen **tsehlt**-plats **fuu**-e tsvey pehr**zoh**nen unt drhey **nehsh**te **boo**chen

how much is it a night?
wie viel kostet das pro Nacht?
vee feel **kos**tet das prhoh nacht?

where is the shower block?
wo sind die Duschen?
voh zint dee **doo**shen?

can we pay, please? we were at space …
können wir bitte bezahlen? wir hatten Platz Nummer …
*keu*nen vee-e **bi**te be**tsaa**len? vee-e **hat**en plats **num**e …

Understanding

es kostet … pro Person und Nacht
it's … per person per night

wenn Sie etwas brauchen, fragen Sie ruhig
if you need anything, just ask

EATING AND DRINKING

For a quick snack, try an **Imbiss**, a German snack bar serving fast food such as grilled sausages and chips. There are also many Turkish snack bars. **Wirtshäuser** and **Gaststätten** are traditional restaurants serving simple food and local specialities. **Restaurants** serve international food as well as some German specialities.

Breakfast (**Frühstück**) in Germany can include bread and pastries, cold meats, cheese, yoghurt, cereal and fruit, accompanied by tea or coffee (which Germans drink a lot of). Lunch (**Mittagessen**) used to be the most important meal of the day, but this is less the case nowadays; many workers simply grab a sandwich. Many restaurants offer a set menu at lunchtime (**Tageskarte**), while dinner is à la carte. In the evening, Germans tend to eat early at home (from about 6pm), but restaurants serve food until 10 or 11pm.

If you order water in a restaurant, you will always be served a bottle of sparkling mineral water unless you specify "**stilles Wasser**" (still water). Service is included and you do not have to leave a tip, but it is polite to round up the total cost if you are happy with the service. Give the tip directly to the waiter or write the amount on your credit card bill, rather than leaving it on the table. If you want the waiter to keep the change, just say "**stimmt so**" (that's fine). If you are in a large group, the waiter will ask if you would like to pay separately (**getrennt**) or together (**zusammen**).

The basics

beer	das Bier *das bee-e*
bill	die Rechnung *dee rhehsh*nung
black coffee	der Kaffee ohne Milch *daye kafay ohne milsh*
bottle	die Flasche *dee fla*she
bread	das Brot *das brhoht*
breakfast	das Frühstück *das frh<u>uu</u>stuuk*
coffee	der Kaffee *daye kafay*
Coke®	die Cola *dee kohla*
dessert	die Nachspeise *dee nach*shpeyze

43

dinner	das Abendessen *das aabent-ehsen*
fruit juice	der Saft *daye saft*
lemonade	die Limonade *dee limohnaade*
lunch	das Mittagessen *das mitaak-ehsen*
main course	das Hauptgericht *das howptgerhicht*
menu	die Speisekarte *dee speyze-kaate*
mineral water	das Mineralwasser *das minehraalvase*
orange juice	der Orangensaft *daye orhangshensaft*
red wine	der Rotwein *daye rhohtveyn*
rosé wine	der Rosé *daye rhohzay*
salad	der Salat *daye zalaat*
sandwich	das Sandwich *das zehntvitsh*
service	die Bedienung *dee bedeenung*
sparkling water	der Sprudel *daye shprhoodel*
sparkling wine	der Sekt *daye zehkt*
starter	die Vorspeise *dee fohe-speyze*
still water	das stille Wasser *das shtile vase*
tea	der Tee *daye tay*
tip	das Trinkgeld *das trhinkgehlt*
water	das Wasser *das vase*
white coffee	der Kaffee mit Milch *daye kafay mit milsh*
white wine	der Weißwein *daye veysveyn*
wine	der Wein *daye veyn*
wine list	die Weinkarte *dee veynkaate*
to eat	essen *ehsen*
to have breakfast	frühstücken *frhuustuuken*
to have dinner	zu Abend essen *tsoo aabent ehsen*
to have lunch	zu Mittag essen *tsoo mitaak ehsen*
to order	bestellen *beshtehlen*

Expressing yourself

shall we go and have something to eat?
sollen wir essen gehen?
zolen vee-e ehsen gayen?

do you want to go for a drink?
möchten Sie etwas trinken gehen?
meushten zee ehtvas trhinken gayen?

can you recommend a good restaurant?
wissen Sie ein gutes Restaurant?
*visen zee eyn goot*es rhehstohrhon

I'm not very hungry
ich habe keinen großen Hunger
*ish haab*e *key*nen *grhoh*sen *hung*e

excuse me! *(to call the waiter)*
Entschuldigung!
*ehntshul*digung!

cheers!
Prost!
prhohst!

that was lovely
es war sehr lecker
ehs vaa zaye **leh**ke

could you bring us an ashtray, please?
könnten Sie uns bitte einen Aschenbecher bringen?
*keun*ten zee uns **bi**te eynen *a*shenbehshe *brhing*en?

where are the toilets, please?
entschuldigen Sie, wo ist die Toilette?
*ehntshul*digen zee, voh ist dee twa*leh*te?

Understanding

durchgehend warme Küche
Montag Ruhetag

hot food served all day
closed on Mondays

tut mir Leid, die Küche ist schon geschlossen
I'm sorry, we've stopped serving food

RESERVING A TABLE

Expressing yourself

I'd like to reserve a table for tomorrow evening
ich möchte einen Tisch für morgen Abend reservieren
*ish meush*te eynen tish *fuu*-e *mor*gen *aa*bent rhehzehr*vee*rhen

for two people
für zwei Personen
fuu-e tsvey pehr**zoh**nen

around 8 o'clock
für acht Uhr
fuu-e acht oo-e

do you have a table available any earlier than that?
haben Sie schon früher einen Tisch frei?
haaben zee shohn frhuue eynen tish frhey?

I've reserved a table – the name's …
ich habe reserviert – auf den Namen …
ish haabe rhehzehrveert – owf dayn naamen …

Understanding

reserviert reserved	**für wie viel Uhr?** for what time?
für wie viele Personen? for how many people?	**auf welchen Namen?** what's the name?
Raucher oder Nichtraucher? smoking or non-smoking?	**haben Sie reserviert?** do you have a reservation?

ist Ihnen dieser Tisch hier recht?
is this table all right for you?

tut mir Leid, im Moment ist nichts frei
I'm afraid we're full at the moment

ORDERING FOOD

Expressing yourself

we're ready to order
wir würden gerne bestellen
vee-e vuurden gehrne beshtehlen

could you give us a few more minutes?
wir brauchen noch ein paar Minuten
vee-e brhowchen noch eyn paa minooten

I'd like … ich möchte … *ish meushte …*	**could I have …?** könnte ich … bekommen? *keunte ish … bekomen?*

EATING AND DRINKING

could you tell me what Sauerbraten is?
was ist denn bitte Sauerbraten?
vas ist dehn bite zowe-brhaaten?

I'll have that
ich nehme das
ish nayme das

does it come with vegetables?
wird Gemüse dazu serviert?
virt gemuuze datsoo zehrveert?

what are today's specials?
welche Tagesgerichte gibt es?
vehlshe taages-gerhishte geept ehs?

what desserts do you have?
was für Nachspeisen haben Sie?
vas fuu-e nachshpeyzen haaben zee?

a bottle of red/white wine
eine Flasche Rotwein/Weißwein
eyne flashe rhoht-veyn/veys-veyn

that's for me
das ist für mich
das ist fuu-e mish

a glass/bottle of water, please
ein Glas/eine Flasche Wasser bitte
eyn glaas/eyne flashe vase bite

this isn't what I ordered, I wanted …
das habe ich nicht bestellt, ich wollte …
das haabe ish nisht beshtehlt, ish volte …

could we have some more bread, please?
könnten wir bitte noch etwas Brot haben?
keunten vee-e bite noch ehtvas brhoht haaben?

could we have some salt and pepper, please?
könnten wir bitte Salz und Pfeffer haben?
keunten vee-e bite zalts unt pfehfe haaben?

Understanding

möchten Sie bestellen?
are you ready to order?

ich komme gleich noch einmal
I'll come back in a few minutes

was möchten Sie trinken?
what would you like to drink?

hat es geschmeckt?
was everything all right?

tut mir Leid, … ist aus
I'm sorry, we don't have any… left

möchten Sie eine Nachspeise oder Kaffee?
would you like dessert or coffee?

BARS AND CAFÉS

Germany produces some very good wines, mainly white, grown in various regions. It is usual to have a glass of white wine or **Sekt** (sparkling wine) as an apéritif before dinner. Wine bars (**Weinstube** or **Weinkeller**) can be found in all towns; they also serve hot snacks.

Schnaps (a type of strong spirit) is usually drunk after a meal or as a chaser with beer. Every region has its own special spirit, including cherry or raspberry spirit, plum brandy, **Weinbrand** (brandy) and **Kümmel** (caraway-flavoured, from the Baltic coast).

Beer is easily the most popular drink in Germany. With over 1,250 breweries and 500 different brands, the Germans are the second-biggest beer drinkers in the world (after the Czechs). Some beers which stand out are: **Altbier** (amber-coloured beer served in small glasses of 0.2 l – around a third of a pint – in the Düsseldorf region); **Berliner Weiße** (wheat beer from Berlin which is light, fizzy and slightly bitter); **Kölsch** (clear, flavoursome beer from Cologne, served in glasses called **Stangen**); **Pils** or **Pilsener** (lager served all over Germany, with a rich froth); **Weizenbier** (wheat beer sometimes served with a slice of lemon) – in Bavaria this is called **Weißbier** and is served in quantities of 1 litre (**eine Maß**) or 0.5 litre (**eine halbe Maß**).

Lemonade shandy is called **Radler** (**Alsterwasser** in northern Germany). Sparkling mineral water is often mixed with apple juice (**Apfelsaftschorle**), orange juice (**Orangensaftschorle**), white wine (**Weißweinschorle**) or red wine (**Rotweinschorle**).

Expressing yourself

I'd like …
ich möchte …
ish meushte …

a Coke®/a diet Coke®
eine Cola/eine Cola Light
eyne kohla/eyne kohla leyt

a glass of white/red wine
ein Glas Weißwein/Rotwein
*eyn glaas **veys**-veyn/**rhoht**-veyn*

a black/white coffee
einen Kaffee ohne Milch/mit Milch
*eynen **kafay** ohne milsh/mit milsh*

a cup of tea
einen Tee
eynen tay

a coffee and a croissant
einen Kaffee und ein Croissant
*eynen **kafay** unt eyn krhwa**son***

a cup of hot chocolate (with cream)
eine heiße Schokolade (mit Sahne)
*eyne **heyse** shokoh**laade** (mit **zaa**ne)*

the same again, please
noch ein ... bitte
*noch eyn ... **bit**e*

could I have some milk with my tea?
könnte ich bitte etwas Milch zum Tee haben?
*keunte ish **bit**e ehtvas milsh tsum tay **haa**ben?*

Understanding

alkoholfrei
non-alcoholic

was kann ich Ihnen bringen?
what would you like?

hier ist Nichtraucher
this is the non-smoking area

könnte ich bitte kassieren?
could I ask you to pay now, please?

Some informal expressions

voll (bis oben hin) sein to be full up
einen Schwips haben to be tipsy
einen Kater haben to have a hangover

EATING AND DRINKING

THE BILL

Expressing yourself

the bill, please
die Rechnung bitte
dee rhehshnung bite

I had ... *(when splitting the bill)*
ich zahle ...
ish tsaale ...

I think there's a mistake in the bill
ich glaube, Sie haben etwas falsch berechnet
ish glowbe, zee haaben ehtvas falsh berhehshnet

how much do I owe you?
was macht das?
vas macht das?

do you take credit cards?
kann ich mit Kreditkarte bezahlen?
kan ish mit krhehdeetkaate betsaalen?

Understanding

zusammen oder getrennt?
are you paying together or separately?

nein, wir nehmen leider keine Kreditkarten
no, I'm afraid we don't accept credit cards

FOOD AND DRINK

Understanding

am Stück	unsliced
blutig	rare
frittiert	deep-fried
gebraten	fried; roast
gedünstet	steamed
gefüllt	stuffed
gegrillt	grilled
gekocht	boiled
geräuchert	smoked
geschmolzen	melted
geschmort	braised
gewürzt	spicy
gut durchgebraten	well done
im Holzofen gebacken	baked in a wood-burning stove
im Ofen gebacken	oven-baked/-roasted
in Scheiben	sliced
kalt	cold
knusprig	crisp
luftgetrocknet	air-dried
paniert	in breadcrumbs
-püree	puree
sautiert	sauté
scharf	hot, very spicy

Vorspeisen starters

Badischer Fleischsalat	salad of strips of sausage, gherkins, etc in a mayonnaise dressing
Bismarckhering in Senfsoße	filleted pickled herring in mustard sauce
Kieler Sprotten	smoked sprats
Krabben-Avocado-Cocktail	prawn and avocado cocktail
Schupfnudeln mit Apfelmus	small potato dumplings with apple sauce
Zwiebelkuchen mit Speck	onion tart with diced bacon

Suppen soups

Soups are often served as a starter or eaten as a snack. If you visit in the spring, you should try the light, tasty **Spargelcremesuppe** (cream of asparagus soup). **Gulaschsuppe**, a Hungarian soup made with beef, onions and paprika, is a delicious, warming winter dish.

Aalsuppe	eel soup
Bohnensuppe	bean soup
Dinkelsuppe	spelt soup *(wheat-like grain)*
Fischsuppe	fish soup
Fliederbeersuppe	elderberry soup
Gemüseeintopf	vegetable stew
Gulaschsuppe	goulash soup
Kartoffelsuppe	potato soup
Krabbensuppe	prawn soup
Kräuterrahmsuppe	cream of herb soup
Leberknödelsuppe	liver dumpling soup
Ochsenschwanzsuppe	oxtail soup
Spargelcremesuppe	cream of asparagus soup
Tomatensuppe	tomato soup

Fleisch meat

Bohneneintopf mit Fleisch	bean stew with meat
Brathuhn	roast chicken
Eisbein	knuckle of pork
Fasan auf Sauerkraut	pheasant on a bed of sauerkraut
Fleischkäse	spiced meat loaf
Gebratene Taube	roast pigeon
Hasenkeule in Preiselbeersahne	leg of hare in cranberry cream sauce
Hasenpfeffer	spicy hare stew
Hirschragout	ragout of venison
Hühnerfrikassee	chicken fricassee
Kalbsgeschnetzeltes	fried thin strips of veal

Kalbshaxe	knuckle of veal
Kalbsleber	calves' liver
Kalbsnierenbraten	roast veal wrapped around calves' kidneys
Kalbsschnitzel	veal cutlet
Kalbsschulter in Pilzsoße	shoulder of veal in mushroom sauce
Kasseler mit Sauerkraut	smoked loin of pork with sauerkraut
Königsberger Klopse	meatballs in caper sauce
Lammkeule mit Knoblauch und Minze	leg of lamb with garlic and mint
Lammschulter	shoulder of lamb
Leberkäse	spiced meat loaf
Maultaschen	ravioli
Ochsenbrust	breast of ox
paniertes Schnitzel	cutlet in breadcrumbs
Putenschnitzel	turkey cutlet
Rehbraten	roast venison
Rehmedaillons mit Sauerkirschen	venison medallions with sour cherries
Rinderbraten	roast beef
Rinderrouladen	beef olives
Schmorbraten	braised beef
Schmorkaninchen	braised rabbit
Schnitzel mit Jägersoße	pork cutlet in a spicy mushroom sauce
Schweinebraten	roast pork
Schweinerippchen	lightly smoked pork chop
Tafelspitz mit Meerrettichsahne	boiled beef with horseradish sauce
Wiener Schnitzel	veal cutlet in breadcrumbs
Wildgulasch mit Pilzen	game goulash with mushrooms
Wildschweinragout	ragout of wild boar

Wurst sausages

Bierwurst	cold sausage traditionally eaten with beer *(eaten sliced on bread)*
Blutwurst	black pudding *(eaten sliced on bread)*
Bockwurst	boiled pork sausage *(eaten unsliced and usually in a bread roll with mustard)*

Bratwurst	fried pork sausage *(eaten unsliced)*
Currywurst	slices of fried pork sausage with curry sauce
Leberwurst	liver sausage *(for spreading)*
Schinkenwurst	ham sausage *(eaten sliced on bread)*
Weißwurst	boiled veal sausage *(eaten unsliced)*
Wiener (Würstchen)	frankfurter *(eaten unsliced)*

Fisch fish

The greatest variety of fish is found in Northern Germany (Schleswig-Holstein, near the Baltic Sea). Freshwater fish (some of them farmed) are available all over the country. Raw and pickled fish are popular.

Aal blau	boiled eel
Aal in Dillsobe	eel in dill sauce
Aal in Kräutersoße	eel in herb sauce
Fischfilets mit Kartoffelpüree	fish fillets with mashed potatoes
Forelle blau	boiled trout
Forelle Müllerin	trout covered in flour and fried in butter
Gebratene Scholle	fried plaice
Hecht grün	pike with herb sauce
Hecht in Rahmsoße	pike in cream sauce
Kabeljaufilet	cod fillet
Karpfen blau	boiled carp
Matjesfilets mit Zwiebelringen	young salted herrings with onion rings
Schollenfilets in Speckmantel	plaice fillets wrapped in bacon slices
Seezungenröllchen	rolled fillets of sole
Zander in Rote-Beete-Soße	zander in beetroot sauce

FOOD AND DRINK

Gemüse vegetables

When you order a main meal of meat or fish in a restaurant, it will usually be served with vegetables. Potatoes (in all forms) are a very popular accompaniment, but you will also find rice and pasta on offer. Cabbage (white and red, as well as kale), carrots, peas, green beans or a salad might also be on the menu. **Sauerkraut**, an Alsatian speciality, is not as common in Germany as many people think.

Blumenkohl	cauliflower
Bratkartoffeln	fried potatoes
Erbsen	peas
grüne Bohnen	green beans
Grünkohl	kale
Karotten	carrots
Kartoffeln	potatoes
Kohl	cabbage
Linsen	lentils
Möhren	carrots
Nudeln	pasta
Pellkartoffeln	boiled potatoes *(cooked and sometimes served in their skins)*
Pommes frites	chips
Reis	rice
Rote Beete	beetroot
Rotkohl/Rotkraut	red cabbage
Salat	salad
Salzkartoffeln	boiled potatoes
Sauerkraut	sauerkraut
Sellerie	celery
Spargel	asparagus
Tomaten	tomatoes
Weißkohl	white cabbage
Wirsing	savoy cabbage

FOOD AND DRINK

Salate salads

Bohnensalat	green bean salad
Gemischter Salat	mixed salad
Grüner Salat	green salad
Joghurtdressing	yoghurt dressing
Kartoffelsalat	potato salad
Nizza-Salat	salad of olives, tomatoes, anchovies, hard-boiled eggs etc
Rote-Beete-Salat	beetroot salad
Vinaigrette	oil-and-vinegar dressing

Kuchen und Nachspeisen cakes and desserts

Each region has its own dessert specialities, and there is a wide variety of delicious cakes. When it's time for **Kaffee und Kuchen** (afternoon tea), you could try a **Strudel** (a thin pastry roll with a fruit filling) or a piece of **Schwarzwälder Kirschtorte** (Black Forest gateau, a rich chocolate cake filled and topped with black cherries and cream). A **Kuchen** is a large, firm, flour-based cake baked in a round, rectangular or ring-shaped tin. A **Torte** is a high, round gateau, filled with cream and sometimes topped with fruit. **Stückchen** or **Teilchen** are small cakes and pastries.

Apfel im Schlafrock	baked apple in pastry
Apfelkuchen	apple cake
Apfelpfannkuchen	apple pancake
Apfelstrudel	thin pastry roll with apple filling
Bayerische Creme mit Früchten	thick vanilla cream dessert with fruit
Bratäpfel	baked apples
Erdbeertorte	strawberry gateau
Frankfurter Kranz	ring-shaped cake filled with cream and almond praline
Gemischtes Eis	mixed ice cream
Heidelbeerpfannkuchen	bilberry pancake

Karottenkuchen	carrot cake
Kartoffelpuffer mit Apfelmus	potato pancakes *(made from grated potatoes)* with apple sauce
Käsekuchen	cheesecake
Käse-Sahne-Torte	soft cheese and cream gateau
Mohnkuchen	poppy-seed cake
Obstsalat mit Joghurtsoße	fruit salad with yoghurt sauce
Rhabarbergrütze	jelly-like dessert made of rhubarb, fruit juice and sugar
Rote Grütze	jelly-like dessert made of red berries, fruit juice and sugar
Rumpudding	blancmange-like dessert with rum
Sauerkirschen mit Grießnocken	sour cherries with small semolina dumplings
Waffel mit Schlagsahne	waffle with whipped cream

Imbiss on the go

Belegtes Brötchen mit Käse	cheese roll
Belegtes Brötchen mit Schinken	ham roll
Brezel	pretzel
Currywurst mit Pommes	slices of fried pork sausage with curry sauce and chips
Döner-Kebab	doner kebab *(spicy grilled meat with salad and garlic sauce in pitta bread)*
Fischbrötchen	fish roll
Frikadellen mit Kartoffelsalat	meatballs with potato salad
Halbes Hähnchen	half a roast chicken
Handkäse mit Musik	small, round, strong cheese containing caraway, in a marinade of vinegar, oil, onion and pepper
Laugenbrötchen mit Butter	pretzel roll and butter
Rührei mit Speck	scrambled eggs with diced bacon
Spiegelei	fried egg
Strammer Max	fried egg and ham on bread
Wiener Würstchen mit Kartoffelsalat	frankfurters with potato salad

GLOSSARY OF FOOD AND DRINK

Aal eel
Abendessen evening meal
Apfel apple
Apfelmost apple juice; cider
Apfelsaft apple juice
Artischocke artichoke
Auflauf bake
Austern oysters
Avocado avocado
Banane banana
Bärlauch wild garlic
Barsch perch
Basilikum basil
Bataviasalat Batavia lettuce *(type of crisp, curly lettuce)*
Beilage side dish
Berliner jam-filled doughnut
Bier beer
Birne pear
Birnengeist spirit made from pears
Biskuit sponge cake
Bitterschokolade plain chocolate
Blätterteig puff pastry
brauner Zucker brown sugar
Brombeere blackberry
Brot bread
Brötchen bread roll
Brunnenkresse watercress
Butter butter
Calamares deep-fried squid rings
Cayennepfeffer cayenne
Champignon mushroom
Chicoree chicory
Dattel date
Dill dill
Dinkel spelt *(wheat-like grain)*

Eintopf stew
Eis ice cream
Endiviensalat endive salad
Erdbeere strawberry
Erdnuss peanut
Erdnussbutter peanut butter
Espresso espresso
Essig vinegar
Essiggurke pickled gherkin
Estragon tarragon
Fasan pheasant
Feldsalat lamb's lettuce
Fenchel fennel
Fencheltee fennel tea
fettarme Milch semi-skimmed milk
Filet fillet
Fleisch meat
Forelle trout
Frischkäse soft cream cheese
Frischmilch fresh milk
Frühlingszwiebel spring onion
Frühstück breakfast
Frühstücksei boiled egg *(for breakfast)*
Gans goose
Garnele shrimp
Geflügel poultry
gekochter Schinken cooked ham
Gelee jelly
Gemüseeintopf vegetable stew
Geschnetzeltes thin strips of meat
Getränke drinks
Getreide grain
Glühwein mulled wine

Goldbrasse sea bream
Grapefruitsaft grapefruit juice
Grog hot toddy
grüne Bohnen green beans
grüner Pfeffer green pepper *(spice)*
grüner Tee green tea
Grünkern wheat-like grain harvested while still green
Grünkohl kale
Gulaschsuppe goulash soup
Gurke cucumber; gherkin
Hackfleisch mince
Hacksteak fried steak made of mince
Haferflocken rolled oats
Hagebuttentee rosehip tea
Halbfettstufe medium-fat
hartgekochtes Ei hard-boiled egg
Hase hare
Haselnuss hazelnut
Hecht pike
Hefezopf yeast plait *(loaf)*
Heidelbeere bilberry
Heilbutt halibut
Hering herring
Himbeere raspberry
Hirsch venison
H-Milch long-life milk
Honig honey
Honigmelone honeydew melon
Hopfen hops
Huhn chicken
Hühnerbrust chicken breast
Hühnerkeule chicken leg
Hühnerleber chicken liver
Hummer lobster
Hüttenkäse cottage cheese
Ingwer ginger

Innereien offal
Jägersoße spicy mushroom sauce
Jakobsmuschel scallop
Joghurt yoghurt
Kabeljaufilet cod fillet
Kaffee coffee
Kalb(sfleisch) veal
Kamillentee camomile tea
Kaninchen rabbit
Kaper caper
Karamell caramel
Karotten carrots
Karpfen carp
Kartoffeln potatoes
Kartoffelpüree mashed potatoes
Käse cheese
Keks biscuit
Kerbel chervil
Kirsche cherry
Kirschwasser kirsch *(spirit made from cherries)*
Knoblauch garlic
koffeinfreier Kaffee decaffeinated coffee
Kognak brandy
Kohl cabbage
Kohlrabi kohlrabi *(turnip-like vegetable)*
Kokosnuss coconut
Kopfsalat lettuce
Koriander coriander
Korinthe currant
Kornschnaps spirit made from grain
Krabbe prawn
Kräuter herbs
Kräutertee herbal tea
Kuchen cake
Kümmel caraway

Kürbis pumpkin
Lachs salmon
Lamm lamb
Lammkeule leg of lamb
Lammschulter shoulder of lamb
Landjäger type of spicy smoked
  sausage
Languste crayfish
Lauch leeks
Leber liver
Leitungswasser tap water
Limette lime
Limonade fizzy drink; lemonade
Lokum Turkish delight
Lorbeerblatt bay leaf
Magenbitter bitters
Magerstufe low-fat
Magermilch skimmed milk
Mais sweetcorn
Maiskolben corn on the cob
Majoran marjoram
Makrele mackerel
Mandel almond
Mangold mangel-wurzel
Maracuja passion fruit
Margarine margarine
Marmelade jam
Maultaschen ravioli
Mehl flour
Melone melon
Meerrettich horseradish
Miesmuschel mussel
Milch milk
Milchshake milk shake
Mineralwasser mineral water
Minze mint
Mirabelle mirabelle *(small yellow
  plum)*

Mirabellenschnaps spirit made
  from mirabelles
Mischbrot rye-and-wheat bread
Mittagessen lunch
Mohn poppy seeds
Mohnkuchen poppy-seed cake
Möhren carrots
Mürbeteig shortcrust pastry
Muskatnuss nutmeg
Nektarine nectarine
Nelke clove
Niere kidney
Nudeln pasta
Nüsse nuts
Obst fruit
Obstkuchen fruit flan
Obstwasser spirit made from fruit
Ochsenbrust ox breast
Ochsenschwanz oxtail
Ofenkartoffel baked potato
Okra okra
Öl oil
Olive olive
Olivenöl olive oil
Orange orange
Orangenlimonade orangeade
Orangensaft orange juice
Oregano oregano
Pampelmuse grapefruit
paniertes Schnitzel cutlet in
  breadcrumbs
Paprika *(vegetable)* pepper; *(spice)*
  paprika
Parmaschinken Parma ham
Pastete pâté; vol-au-vent
Pekannuss pecan
Pellkartoffeln boiled potatoes
  *(cooked and sometimes served in
  their skins)*

Peperoni chilli *(vegetable)*
Perlhuhn guinea fowl
Pesto pesto
Petersilie parsley
Pfannkuchen pancake
Pfirsich peach
Pflaume plum
Pils lager
Pilz mushroom
Pistazie pistachio
Pommes frites chips
Portwein port
Pudding blancmange-like dessert
Puderzucker icing sugar
Quittengelee quince jelly
Räucherlachs smoked salmon
Räucherschinken smoked ham
Reh venison
Rehbraten roast venison
Reis rice
Rettich radish *(large white or red variety)*
Rhabarber rhubarb
Rinderfilet fillet of beef
Rind(fleisch) beef
Rindersteak beefsteak
Rippchen lightly smoked pork chop
Rochen ray *(fish)*
roher Schinken cured ham
Roggen rye
Rohrzucker cane sugar
Romanasalat cos lettuce
Rosenkohl Brussels sprouts
Rosine raisin
Rosmarin rosemary
Rotbarbe red mullet
Rote Beete beetroot

rote Johannisbeere redcurrant
Rotwein red wine
Rucola rocket
Rührei scrambled eggs
Rum rum
Rumpsteak rumpsteak
Sachertorte type of rich chocolate cake
Safran saffron
Saft juice
Salat salad
Salbei sage
Salz salt
Salzkartoffeln boiled potatoes
Sardelle anchovy
Sauerkirsche sour cherry
Sauerrahm soured cream
saure Sahne soured cream
Schafskäse sheep's cheese
Schalotte shallot
Schaumwein sparkling wine
Schinken ham
Schlagsahne whipping cream; whipped cream
Schnaps schnaps *(type of strong spirit)*
Schnittlauch chives
Schokolade chocolate
Schokoriegel chocolate bar
Scholle plaice
Schwarzbrot dark coarse rye bread
schwarze Johannisbeere blackcurrant
schwarzer Pfeffer black pepper
Schwarztee black tea
Schweinebraten roast pork
Schwein(efleisch) pork

Schweinerippchen lightly smoked pork chop
Schwertfisch swordfish
Seelachs pollack *(fish)*
Seeteufel monkfish
Sekt sparkling wine *(similar to champagne)*
Sellerie celery
Senf mustard
Sesam sesame seeds
Sojasprossen beansprouts
Sonnenblumenkerne sunflower seeds
Sonnenblumenöl sunflower oil
Sorbet sorbet
Spargel asparagus
Spargelcremesuppe cream of asparagus soup
Sprotte sprat
Sprudel sparkling mineral water
Stachelbeere gooseberry
Steinpilz cep *(type of brown-capped mushroom)*
Stockfisch stockfish
Streichkäse cheese spread
Streusel crumble topping
Sultanine sultana
süße Sahne whipping cream
süßer Senf mild, slightly sweet mustard
Tee tea
Thunfisch tuna
Tintenfisch squid
Tomate tomato
Torte gateau
Traube grape
Trüffel truffle
Vanille vanilla

Vollmilch full-fat milk
Vollmilchschokolade milk chocolate
Waffel waffle
Waldmeisterbowle fruit punch flavoured with the plant woodruff
Walnuss walnut
Wasser water
Wassermelone watermelon
Weißbier wheat beer
Weißbrot white bread
weißer Pfeffer white pepper
Weißkohl white cabbage
Weißwein white wine
Wein wine
Weinbrand brandy
Weizen wheat
Weizenbier wheat beer
Wiener Würstchen frankfurter
Wild game
Wildschwein wild boar
Wurst sausage
Würstchen thin sausage *(frankfurter-style or fried pork sausage, eaten unsliced)*
Zander zander
Zartbitterschokolade plain chocolate
Ziegenkäse goat's cheese
Zimt cinnamon
Zitrone lemon
Zitronenlimonade lemonade
Zucchini courgette
Zucker sugar
Zwetschge plum
Zwiebel onion
Zwiebelringe onion rings

You can find out what is on in cultural magazines or local newspapers, which can be found in tourist information centres and theatres as well as cafés and other public places. It is not usually necessary to book very far in advance, and there are always student discounts available.

The popularity of local theatre troupes means that most towns have their own busy programme of theatrical and musical events. Besides classical music, Germany has lively rock and jazz scenes, with concerts held in clubs, bars and small 'alternative' venues.

Going to the cinema costs about the same as in the UK. Most cinemas have their own half-price day (**Kinotag**) once a week. International films are widely shown, but are usually dubbed into German. Films showing in the original language with subtitles are marked **OmU** (**Original mit Untertiteln**), while those without subtitles are marked **OF** (**Originalfassung**) or **OV** (**Originalversion**).

When meeting friends, people usually go to a bar or café rather than to someone's house. There are international-style bars in all the big cities, but many Germans prefer to go to a more traditional establishment serving beer (**Bierlokal**) or wine (**Weinstube**). If you are invited out with people, you should make an effort to arrive on time: Germans tend to be punctual.

Germany is famous for its nightclubs. These tend to play mainly techno in the cities, but you can find more traditional local music in smaller towns. There are many stylish and unusual clubs, housed in places like old factories or aircraft hangars. Sometimes admission includes a free drink. Clubs close between 1 and 3am, or later in Berlin and Leipzig.

The basics

ballet	das Ballett *das baleht*
band	die Band *dee behnt*
bar	die Bar *dee baa*

cinema	das Kino *das keenoh*
circus	der Zirkus *daye tsirkus*
classical music	die klassische Musik *dee klasishe moozeek*
club	die Disko *dee diskoh*
concert	das Konzert *das kontsehrt*
dubbed film	der synchronisierte Film *daye zuunkrhohnizeerte film*
festival	das Festival *das fehstivel*
film	der Film *daye film*
folk music	die Volksmusik *dee folksmooseek*
group	die Gruppe *dee grhupe*
jazz	der Jazz *daye jehz*
modern dance	der Modern Dance *daye modehrn dehns*
musical	das Musical *das myoozikel*
party	die Party *dee paati*
play	das Stück *das shtuuk*
pop music	die Popmusik *dee popmooseek*
rock music	die Rockmusik *dee rhokmooseek*
show	die Show *dee shoh*
subtitled film	der Film mit Untertiteln *daye film mit unteteeteln*
theatre	das Theater *das tayaate*
ticket	die Karte *dee kaate*
to book tickets	die Karten vorbestellen *dee kaaten fohebeshtehlen*
to go out	ausgehen *owsgayen*

SUGGESTIONS AND INVITATIONS

Expressing yourself

what do you want to do?
was möchten Sie machen?
vas meushten zee machen?

shall we go for a drink?
sollen wir etwas trinken gehen?
zolen vee-e ehtvas trhinken gayen?

what are you doing tonight?
was machen Sie heute Abend?
vas machen zee hoyte aabent?

do you have plans?
haben Sie schon etwas vor?
haaben zee shohn ehtvas fohe?

would you like to …?
möchten Sie …?
meushten zee …?

I'd love to!
sehr gerne!
zaye gehrne!

I can't today, but maybe some other time
heute kann ich nicht, vielleicht ein andermal
hoyte kan ish nisht, feeleysht eyn andemaal

Understanding

hätten Sie Lust …?
would you like to …?

wie wäre es, wenn …?
how about …?

mögen Sie Jazz?
do you like jazz?

ARRANGING TO MEET

Expressing yourself

what time shall we meet?
wann sollen wir uns treffen?
van zolen vee-e uns trhehfen?

where shall we meet?
wo sollen wir uns treffen?
voh zolen vee-e uns trhehfen?

would it be possible to meet a bit later?
könnten wir uns etwas später treffen?
keunten vee-e uns ehtvas shpehte trhehfen?

I have to meet … at nine
ich bin um neun mit … verabredet
ish bin um noyn mit … fehr-aprhaydet

I don't know where it is but I'll find it on the map
ich weiß nicht, wo es ist, aber ich kann auf dem Stadtplan nachsehen
ish veys nisht, voh ehs ist, aabe ish kan owf daym shtatplaan nachzayen

see you tomorrow night
bis morgen Abend
bis morgen aabent

sorry I'm late
entschuldigen Sie die Verspätung
ehntshuldigen zee dee fehrspehtung

I'll meet you later, I have to stop by the hotel first
ich muss erst noch ins Hotel, ich komme dann nach
ish mus ayest noch ins hohtehl, ish kome dan nach

I'll call/text you if there's a change of plan
falls sich etwas ändert, rufe ich an/schicke ich eine SMS
fals zish ehtvas ehndert, rhoofe ish an/shike ish eyne ehs-ehm-ehs

are you going to eat beforehand?
essen Sie vorher etwas?
ehsen zee fohe-haye ehtvas?

Understanding

passt Ihnen das?
is that all right with you?

wir treffen uns dort
I'll meet you there

ich hole Sie gegen acht ab
I'll come and pick you up about 8

wir können uns am Kinoeingang/am Eingang der Post treffen
we can meet outside the cinema/outside the post office

ich gebe Ihnen meine Nummer und Sie rufen mich morgen an
I'll give you my number and you can call me tomorrow

Some informal expressions

etwas essen gehen to go and have something to eat
einen trinken gehen to go for a drink
in die Kneipe gehen to go to the pub

FILMS, SHOWS AND CONCERTS

Expressing yourself

is there a guide to what's on?
gibt es einen Veranstaltungskalender?
geept ehs eynen fehranshtaltungskalehnde?

I'd like three tickets for ...
ich möchte drei Karten für ...
ish meushte dhrey kaaten fuu-e ...

two tickets, please
zwei Karten bitte
tsvey kaaten bite

the film/the band is called …
der Film/die Band heißt …
daye film/dee behnt heyst …

I've seen the trailer
ich habe die Vorschau gesehen
ish haabe dee fohe-show gezayen

what time does the film/the play/the concert start?
wann fängt der Film/das Stück/das Konzert an?
van fehngt daye film/das shtuuk/das kontsehrt an?

I'd like to go and see a musical
ich würde gern in ein Musical gehen
ish vuurde gehrn in eyn myoozikel gayen

I'll find out whether there are still tickets available
ich werde fragen, ob es noch Karten gibt
ish vehrde frhaagen, op ehs noch kaaten geept

do we need to book in advance?
muss man die Karten vorbestellen?
mus man dee kaaten fohe-bestehlen?

how long is the film/the play on for?
wie lange läuft der Film/das Stück?
vee lange loyft daye film/das shtuuk?

are there tickets for another day?
gibt es für einen anderen Tag noch Karten?
geept ehs fuu-e eynen anderhen taak noch kaaten?

I'd like to go to a bar with some live music
ich würde gern in ein Lokal mit Livemusik gehen
ish vuurde gehrn in eyn lohkaal mit leyfmoozeek gayen

are there any free concerts?
gibt es Konzerte, die keinen Eintritt kosten?
geept ehs kontsehrte, dee keynen eyntrhit kosten?

what sort of music is it?
was für Musik ist das?
vas fuu-e moozeek ist das?

Understanding

ab … im Kino	on general release from …
ab … Jahren	suitable only for persons of … years and over

an der Abendkasse	at the door
demnächst	coming soon
Kasse	box office
Matinee	matinée
Programmkino	arthouse cinema
Vorverkauf	advance booking

es ist ein Openairkonzert
it's an open-air concert

er läuft nächste Woche an
it comes out next week

er läuft um 20 Uhr im Odeon
it's on at 8pm at the Odeon

die Vorstellung ist ausverkauft
that showing's sold out

bis … ist alles ausverkauft
it's all booked up until …

man braucht nicht vorzubestellen
there's no need to book in advance

der Film hat sehr gute Kritiken bekommen
the film had very good reviews

das Stück dauert mit Pause eineinhalb Stunden
the play lasts an hour and a half, including the interval

bitte schalten Sie Ihre Handys aus
please turn off your mobile phones

PARTIES AND CLUBS

Expressing yourself

I'm having a little leaving party tonight
ich mache heute Abend eine kleine Abschiedsparty
ish mache hoyte aabent eyne kleyne apsheets-paati

should I bring something to drink?
soll ich etwas zu trinken mitbringen?
zol ish ehtvas tsoo trhinken mitbrhingen?

we could go to a club afterwards
wir könnten hinterher noch tanzen gehen
vee-e keunten hinte-haye noch tantsen gayen

do you have to pay to get in?
kostet es Eintritt?
kostet ehs eyntrhit?

I have to meet someone inside
ich bin drinnen mit jemandem verabredet
*ish bin **drhin**en mit **yay**mandem fehr-**ap**rhaydet*

will you let me back in when I come back?
lassen Sie mich wieder hinein, wenn ich zurückkomme?
*las*en zee mish **vee**de hi**neyn**, vehn ish tsoo**rhuuk**-kome?*

the DJ's really cool
der DJ ist wirklich toll
*daye **dee**-jay ist **virk**lish tol*

can I buy you a drink?
darf ich Sie zu einem Drink einladen?
*daaf ish zee tsoo **ey**nem drhink **eyn**laaden?*

thanks, but I'm with my boyfriend
nein, danke, ich bin mit meinem Freund hier
*neyn, **dank**e, ish bin mit **mey**nem frhoynt hee-e*

no thanks, I don't smoke
nein, danke, ich rauche nicht
*neyn, **dank**e, ish **row**che nisht*

Understanding

Freigetränk	free drink
Garderobe	cloakroom

Christina macht eine Party	**möchten Sie tanzen?**
there's a party at Christina's place	do you want to dance?
haben Sie Feuer?	**kann ich Sie nach Hause bringen?**
have you got a light?	can I see you home?

darf ich Sie zu einem Drink einladen?
can I buy you a drink?

hätten Sie eine Zigarette für mich?
have you got a cigarette?

ich würde Sie gerne wiedersehen
can we see each other again?

TOURISM AND SIGHTSEEING

German tourist information centres are very efficient. The German National Tourist Board (**Deutsche Zentrale für Tourismus**) is based in Frankfurt am Main (see the Useful Addresses chapter). Local tourist offices are open from Monday to Saturday, and sometimes on Sundays in big cities. They all sell maps, guides and passes for public transport, as well as offering tours and cultural events. You will also find local street maps displayed in the street.

Museums in Germany are closed on Mondays. They offer guided tours or headsets, and many also have a café. There are discounts for students and pensioners on presentation of ID. State museums are usually free on Sundays and bank holidays.

The basics

ancient	**alt** *alt*
antique	**antik** *anteek*
area	**die Gegend** *dee gay*gent
castle	(fortress) **die Burg** *dee burk*; (mansion) **das Schloss** *das shlos*
cathedral	**der Dom** *daye dohm*
century	**das Jahrhundert** *das yaahun*dert
church	**die Kirche** *dee kir*she
exhibition	**die Ausstellung** *dee ows-shteh*lung
gallery	**die Galerie** *dee galer*hee
modern art	**die moderne Kunst** *dee mohdehr*ne kunst
monument	**das Denkmal** *das dehnk*maal
mosque	**die Moschee** *dee mo*shay
museum	**das Museum** *das mooza*yum
painting	**das Gemälde** *das gem*ehlde

park	**der Park** *daye park*
ruins	**die Ruinen** *dee rhoo-eenen*
sculpture	**die Skulptur** *dee skulptoo-e*
statue	**die Statue** *dee shtaatoo-e*
street map	**der Stadtplan** *daye shtatplaan*
synagogue	**die Synagoge** *dee zuunagohge*
tour guide	**der Reiseführer** *daye rheyze-fuurhe*
tourist	**der Tourist** *daye toorhist*
tourist information centre	**die Touristeninformation** *dee toorhisten-informatsiohn*
town centre	**das Stadtzentrum** *das shtat-tsehntrum*

Expressing yourself

I'd like some information on …
ich hätte gern Informationen über …
ish hehte gehrn informatsiohnen uube …

can you tell me where the tourist information centre is?
können Sie mir sagen, wo die Touristeninformation ist?
keunen zee mee-e zaagen, voh dee toorhisten-informatsiohn ist?

do you have a street map of the town?
haben Sie einen Stadtplan?
haaben zee eynen shtatplaan?

I was told there's an old abbey you can visit
ich habe gehört, dass es hier eine alte Abtei zu besichtigen gibt
ish haabe geheurt, das ehs hee-e eyne alte aptey tsoo bezishtigen geept

can you show me where it is on the map?
können Sie es mir auf dem Stadtplan zeigen?
keunen zee ehs mee-e owf daym shtatplaan tseygen?

how do you get there?
wie komme ich dorthin?
vee kome ish dorthin?

do you have to pay to get in?
kostet es Eintritt?
kostet ehs eyntrhit?

when was it built?
wann wurde es erbaut?
van vurde ehs ehrbowt?

Understanding

Altstadt	old town
Besichtigung	visit
Burg	castle *(fortress)*
Eintritt frei	admission free
erbaut	built
Führung	guided tour
geöffnet	open
Gedenkstätte	memorial
geschlossen	closed
mittelalterlich	medieval
Münster	cathedral
Rathaus	town hall
römisch	Roman
Schloss	castle *(mansion)*
Sie sind hier	you are here *(on a map)*
Turmbesteigung	ascent of the tower

die nächste Führung beginnt um 14 Uhr
the next guided tour starts at 2 o'clock

MUSEUMS, EXHIBITIONS AND MONUMENTS

Expressing yourself

I've heard there's a very good exhibition on at the moment
ich habe gehört, es gibt gerade eine gute Ausstellung
ish haabe geheurt, ehs geept gerhaade eyne goote ows-shtehlung

how much is it to get in?
wie viel kostet der Eintritt?
vee feel kostet daye eyntrhit?

is it open on Sundays?
ist es sonntags geöffnet?
ist ehs zontaaks ge-eufnet?

is this ticket valid for the exhibition as well?
gilt diese Karte auch für die Ausstellung?
gilt deeze kaate owch fuu-e dee ows-shtehlung?

are there any discounts for young people?
gibt es eine Ermäßigung für junge Leute?
geept ehs eyne ehrmehsigung fuu-e yunge loyte?

two concessions and one full price, please
zwei ermäßigte Karten und eine normale Karte bitte
tsvey ehrmehsigte kaaten unt eyne normaale kaate bite

I have a student card
ich habe einen Studentenausweis
ish haabe eynen shtoodehnten-owsveys

Understanding

Audioführer	audioguide
Ausgang	exit
Bitte nicht berühren	please do not touch
Bitte Ruhe	silence, please
Fotografieren mit Blitz nicht erlaubt	no flash photography
Fotografieren nicht erlaubt	no photography
Kasse	ticket office
Sonderausstellung	temporary exhibition
ständige Ausstellung	permanent exhibition

das Museum kostet ... Eintritt
admission to the museum costs ...

mit dieser Karte können Sie auch die Ausstellung besuchen
this ticket also gives you admission to the exhibition

haben Sie Ihren Studentenausweis da?
do you have your student card?

GIVING YOUR IMPRESSIONS

Expressing yourself

it's beautiful
es ist wunderschön
ehs ist vunde-sheun

it was beautiful
es war wunderschön
ehs vaa vunde-sheun

it's fantastic
es ist fantastisch
ehs ist fantastish

it was fantastic
es war fantastisch
ehs vaa fantastish

I really enjoyed it
es hat mir sehr gefallen
ehs hat mee-e zaye gefalen

it was a bit boring
es war ein bisschen langweilig
ehs vaa eyn bis-shen langveylish

I didn't like it that much
es hat mir nicht besonders gefallen
ehs hat mee-e nisht bezonders gefalen

I'm not really a fan of modern art
ich mag moderne Kunst nicht besonders
ish maak mohdehrne kunst nisht bezonders

it's expensive for what it is
es ist ganz schön teuer für das, was geboten wird
ehs ist gants sheun toye fuu-e das, vas gebohten virt

it's very touristy
es ist sehr touristisch
ehs ist zaye toorhistish

it was really crowded
es war sehr viel los
ehs vaa zaye feel lohs

we didn't go in the end, the queue was too long
wir sind nicht hineingegangen, die Schlange war zu lang
vee-e zint nicht hineyn-gegangen, dee shlange vaa tsoo lang

we didn't have time to see everything
wir hatten keine Zeit, uns alles anzusehen
vee-e haten keyne tseyt, uns ales an-tsoo-zayen

Understanding

berühmt	famous
malerisch	picturesque
traditionell	traditional
typisch	typical

Sie müssen sich unbedingt ... ansehen
you really must go and see ...

... dürfen Sie auf keinen Fall verpassen
whatever you do, don't miss ...

es ist unbedingt einen Besuch wert
it's definitely worth a visit

man hat einen herrlichen Blick über die Stadt
there's a wonderful view over the city

es ist leider sehr überlaufen
it's become a bit too touristy

SPORTS AND GAMES

Football is the most popular sport in Germany. The best matches are often local, such as those between Munich's **Bayern** and **1860 München**, or between **VFL Bochum** and **Borussia Dortmund**. National league (**Bundesliga**) matches are played at weekends. The season runs from September to June, with breaks over Christmas and in mid-February. Tickets are sold in advance at local agencies.

Tennis has become popular in recent years following the success of Boris Becker and Steffi Graf. Many big cities hold large tournaments throughout the season. Information is available from the German Tennis Federation in Hamburg (tel. 040 411780; www.dtb-tennis.de).

Cycling is possible both in town and in the country (Germany boasts some 35,000 km of cycle paths). Cycling holidays and bike tours are popular, particularly in North Frisia and the Harz Mountains. In cities there are plenty of places that hire out bikes (**Fahrradverleih**).

The main ski resorts are in the German Alps, the most famous one being Garmisch-Partenkirchen. The Harz Mountains also offer good skiing if you prefer somewhere cheaper and less chic. The tourist industry in the Alps is booming, with plenty of tourist offices and hotels.

The basics

ball	der Ball *daye bal*
basketball	Basketball *baaskehtbal*
board game	das Brettspiel *das brhehtshpeel*
cards	die Karten *dee kaaten*
chess	Schach *shach*
cross-country skiing	Langlauf *langlowf*
cycling	Radfahren *rhaatfaarhen*
downhill skiing	Abfahrtslauf *apfaats-lowf*
football	Fußball *foosbal*

golf	Golf *golf*
hiking	Wandern *vandern*
hiking path	der Wanderweg *daye vande-vayk*
match	das Spiel *das shpeel*
mountain biking	Mountainbiking *mowntehnbeyking*
pool	(game) Billard *bilyaat*
rock climbing	Klettern *klehtern*
rollerblading	Inlineskaten *inleyn-skayten*
rugby	Rugby *rhakbee*
skiing	Skifahren *sheefaarhen*
skis	die Skier *dee shee-e*
snowboarding	Snowboarden *snohborden*
sport	der Sport *daye shport*
surfing	Surfen *seurfen*
swimming	Schwimmen *shvimen*
swimming pool	das Schwimmbad *das shvimbaat*
table football	Tischfußball *tishfoosbal*
table tennis	Tischtennis *tishtehnis*
tennis	Tennis *tehnis*
trip	die Tour *dee too-e*
to have a game of ...	eine Runde ... spielen *eyne rhunde ... shpeelen*
to play	spielen *shpeelen*

Expressing yourself

I'd like to hire ... for an hour
ich möchte für eine Stunde ... ausleihen
ish meushte fuu-e eyne shtunde ... ows-leyen

how much is it per person per hour?
wie viel kostet es pro Person und Stunde?
vee feel kostet ehs prhoh pehrzohn unt shtunde?

are there lessons available?
kann man einen Kurs machen?
kan man eynen kurs machen?

I'm not very sporty
ich bin nicht besonders sportlich
ish bin nisht bezonders shportlish

I like swimming/cycling
ich schwimme gern/ich fahre gern Rad
ish shvime gehrn/ish faarhe gehrn rhaat

I'd like to go hiking/mountain biking
ich würde gerne wandern gehen/Mountainbike fahren
ish vuurde gehrne vandern gayen/mowntehnbeyk faarhen

I've never done it before
ich habe das noch nie gemacht
ish haabe das noch nee gemacht

I'm a beginner
ich bin Anfänger
ish bin anfehnge

I'd like to go and watch a football match
ich würde gerne ein Fußballspiel ansehen
ish vuurde gehrne eyn foosbal-shpeel anzayen

we played …
wir haben … gespielt
vee-e haaben … geshpeelt

Understanding

… verleih
… for hire

sind Sie Anfänger?
are you a beginner?

Sie müssen eine Kaution in Höhe von … bezahlen
there is a deposit of …

Sie müssen eine Versicherung abschließen; sie kostet …
insurance is compulsory and costs …

HIKING

Expressing yourself

are there any hiking paths around here?
gibt es hier in der Nähe Wanderwege?
geept ehs hee-e in daye nehe vande-vayge?

can you recommend any good walks in the area?
können Sie eine schöne Wanderung in der Gegend empfehlen?
keunen zee eyne sheune vanderhung in daye gaygent ehmpfaylen?

I've heard there's a nice walk by the lake
ich habe gehört, dass es eine schöne Wanderung am See entlang gibt
ish haabe geheurt, das ehs eyne sheune vanderhung am zay ehntlang geept

we're looking for a short walk somewhere round here
wir möchten hier in der Gegend eine kurze Wanderung machen
vee-e mueshten hee-e in daye gaygent eyne kurtse vanderhung machen

how long does the hike take?
wie lange dauert die Wanderung?
vee lange dowert dee vanderhung?

can I hire hiking boots?
kann ich Wanderschuhe ausleihen?
kan ish vande-shoo-e ows-leyen?

is the path waymarked?
ist der Weg beschildert?
ist daye vayg beshildert?

where's the start of the path?
wo beginnt der Wanderweg?
voh begint daye vande-wayg?

is it a circular path?
ist es ein Rundweg?
ist ehs eyn rhunt-vayg?

is it steep?
ist es steil?
ist ehs shteyl?

shall we stop and have something to eat?
sollen wir Pause machen und etwas essen?
zolen vee-e powze machen unt ehtvas ehsen?

Understanding

durchschnittliche Dauer
average duration *(of walk)*

die Wanderung dauert mit Pausen etwa drei Stunden
it's about three hours' walk including rest stops

bringen Sie eine Regenjacke und Wanderschuhe mit
bring a waterproof jacket and some walking shoes

SKIING AND SNOWBOARDING

Expressing yourself

I'd like to hire skis, poles and boots
ich möchte Skier, Stöcke und Stiefel ausleihen
ish meushte shee-e, shteuke unt shteefel ows-leyen

I'd like to hire a snowboard
ich möchte ein Snowboard ausleihen
ish meushte eyn snohbord ows-leyen

they're too big/small
sie sind zu groß/klein
zee zint tsoo grhohs/kleyn

a day pass, please
einen Tagespass bitte
eynen taages-pas bite

Understanding

Schlepplift	T-bar, button lift
Sessellift	chair lift
Skilift	ski lift
Skipass	lift pass

OTHER SPORTS

Expressing yourself

where can we hire bikes?
wo können wir Fahrräder ausleihen?
voh keunen vee-e faa-rhehde ows-leyen?

are there any cycle paths around here?
gibt es hier Radwege?
geept ehs hee-e rhaat-vayge?

does anyone have a football?
hat jemand einen Fußball?
hat yaymant eynen foosbal?

which team do you support?
welches ist Ihre Lieblingsmannschaft?
vehlshes ist eerhe leeplings-manshaft?

I support Leeds United
ich bin Leeds-United-Fan
ish bin Leeds-United-fan

is there an open-air swimming pool?
gibt es ein Freibad?
geept ehs eyn frheybaat?

I've never been rock climbing before
ich bin noch nie geklettert
ish bin noch nee geklehtert

I'd like to take beginners' sailing lessons
ich möchte einen Segelkurs für Anfänger machen
ish meushte eynen saygelkurs fuu-e anfehnge machen

I run for half an hour every morning
ich jogge jeden Morgen eine halbe Stunde
ish joge yayden morgen eyne halbe shtunde

what do I do if the kayak capsizes?
was mache ich, wenn der Kajak kentert?
vas mache ish, vehn daye kaayak kehntert?

in der Nähe des Bahnhofs ist ein Squashcenter
there are squash courts not far from the station

der Tennisplatz ist belegt
the tennis court's occupied

sollen wir Federball spielen?
shall we have a game of badminton?

können Sie schwimmen?
can you swim?

spielen Sie Basketball?
do you play basketball?

reiten Sie zum ersten Mal?
is this the first time you've been horse-riding?

INDOOR GAMES

Expressing yourself

shall we have a game of cards?
sollen wir Karten spielen?
zolen vee-e kaaten shpeelen?

does anyone know any good card games?
kennt jemand ein gutes Kartenspiel?
kehnt yaymant eyn gootes kaaten-shpeel?

is anyone up for a game of Monopoly®?
spielt jemand mit Monopoly?
shpeelt yaymant mit monohpolee?

it's your turn
Sie sind dran
zee zint drhan

Understanding

spielen Sie Schach?
can you play chess?

haben Sie ein Kartenspiel?
do you have a pack of cards?

> ### Some informal expressions
>
> **ich bin völlig alle** I'm knackered
> **er hat mich abgezogen** he thrashed me

SHOPPING

Shops are generally open from 9.30am to 8pm on weekdays, and from 9.30am to 4pm (most shops in town centres until 8pm) on Saturdays.

If you visit in December, don't forget to go to a traditional Christmas market, where you can buy handmade crafts and gifts. To warm up, you can have a mug of **Glühwein** (mulled wine flavoured with cinnamon) and gingerbread or a sausage.

Most towns have a weekly market where you can buy local produce (including organic produce) such as fruit, vegetables, cheese, sausages, fish, poultry and bread. Local specialities such as honey might also be on offer.

Some informal expressions

Schnäppchen bargain
gesalzene Preise steep prices
ich bin pleite I'm broke

The basics

baker's	die Bäckerei *dee behkerhey*
butcher's	die Metzgerei *dee mehtsgerhey*
cash desk	die Kasse *dee kase*
cheap	billig *bilish*
checkout	die Kasse *dee kase*
clothes	die Bekleidung *dee bekleydung*
department store	das Kaufhaus *das kowfhows*
expensive	teuer *toye*
grams	Gramm *grham*
greengrocer's	der Obsthändler *daye ohpst-hehndle*
hypermarket	der große Supermarkt *daye grhohse zoope-maakt*

kilo	das Kilo *das keeloh*
present	das Geschenk *das geshehnk*
price	der Preis *daye prheys*
receipt	der Kassenbon *daye kasenbong*
refund	die Erstattung *dee ehrshtatung*
sale(s)	der Ausverkauf *daye owsfehrkowf*
sales assistant	der Verkäufer/die Verkäuferin *daye fehrkoyfe/dee fehrkoyferhin*
shopping centre	das Einkaufszentrum *das eynkowfs-tsehntrum*
souvenir	das Andenken *das andehnken*
supermarket	der Supermarkt *daye zoope-maakt*
to buy	kaufen *kowfen*
to cost	kosten *kosten*
to pay	bezahlen *betsaalen*
to sell	verkaufen *fehrkowfen*
to shop	einkaufen *eynkowfen*

Expressing yourself

is there a supermarket near here?
ist hier in der Nähe ein Supermarkt?
ist hee-e in daye nehe eyn zoope-maakt?

where can I buy cigarettes?
wo kann ich Zigaretten kaufen?
voh kan ish tsigarhehten kowfen?

I'd like …
ich möchte …
ish meushte …

I'm looking for …
ich suche …
ish zooche …

do you sell …?
haben Sie …?
haaben zee …?

how much is this?
wie viel kostet das?
vee feel kostet das?

I haven't got much money
ich habe nicht viel Geld
ish haabe nisht feel gehlt

I haven't got enough money
ich habe nicht genug Geld
ish haabe nisht genook gehlt

that's everything, thanks
danke, das wär's
danke, das vehrs

I'll take it
ich nehme es
ish nayme ehs

SHOPPING

do you know where I might find some …?
wissen Sie, wo ich … bekommen kann?
*visen zee, voh ish … be**kom**en kan?*

can you order it for me?
können Sie es für mich bestellen?
*keunen zee ehs fuu-e mish be**shtehl**en?*

can I have a (plastic) bag?
könnte ich bitte eine Tüte haben?
keunte ish bite eyne tuute haaben?

I think you've made a mistake with my change
ich glaube, Sie haben mir falsch herausgegeben
ish glowbe, zee haaben mee-e falsh hehrhows-gegayben

Understanding

ab … Euro	from … euros
Ausverkauf	sale(s)
Sonderangebot	special offer
Sonntag/13–15 Uhr geschlossen	closed Sundays/1pm to 3pm
von … bis … geöffnet	open from … to …

darf es noch etwas sein?
will there be anything else?

möchten Sie eine Tüte?
would you like a bag?

PAYING

Expressing yourself

where do I pay?
wo kann ich bezahlen?
*voh kan ish be**tsaal**en?*

how much do I owe you?
wie viel macht das?
vee feel macht das?

could you write it down for me, please?
könnten Sie mir das bitte aufschreiben?
keunten zee mee-e das bite owfshrheyben?

can I pay by credit card?
kann ich mit Kreditkarte bezahlen?
kan ish mit krhehdeetkaate betsaalen?

I'll pay in cash
ich zahle bar
ish tsaale baa

I'm sorry, I haven't got any change
tut mir Leid, ich habe es nicht kleiner
toot mee-e leyt, ish haabe ehs nisht kleyne

can I have a written receipt?
kann ich bitte eine Quittung haben?
kan ish bite eyne kvitung haaben?

Understanding

an der Kasse zahlen
pay at the cash desk

eine Unterschrift bitte
could you sign here, please?

zahlen Sie bar oder mit Karte?
are you paying cash or by card?

haben Sie es vielleicht etwas kleiner?
do you have anything smaller?

ich bräuchte einen Ausweis
have you got any ID?

FOOD

Expressing yourself

where can I buy food around here?
wo kann ich hier in der Nähe Lebensmittel kaufen?
voh kan ish hee-e in daye nehe laybens-mitel kowfen?

is there a market?
gibt es einen Markt?
geept ehs eynen maakt?

is there a baker's around here?
ist hier in der Nähe eine Bäckerei?
ist hee-e in daye nehe eyne behkerhey?

it's for four people
für vier Personen
fuu-e fee-e pehrzohnen

about 300 grams
ungefähr dreihundert Gramm
ungefeh-e drhey-hundert grham

a kilo of apples, please
ein Kilo Äpfel bitte
eyn keeloh ehpfel bite

a bit less/more
ein bisschen weniger/mehr
eyn bis-shen vaynige/maye

can I taste the cheese?
kann ich den Käse probieren?
kan ish dayn kehze prhohbeeren?

does it keep well?
hält sich das eine Weile?
hehlt zish das eyne veyle?

I'm looking for cereals
wo finde ich Müsli und Ähnliches?
voh finde ish muusli unt ehnlishes?

I'd like five slices of ham
ich möchte fünf Scheiben Schinken
ish meushte fuunf sheyben shinken

I'd like some of that goat's cheese
ich hätte gern ein Stück von diesem Ziegenkäse
ish hehte gehrn eyn shtuuk fon deezem tseegen-kehze

Understanding

Bio-	organic
Feinkostgeschäft	delicatessen
hausgemacht	homemade
mindestens haltbar bis ...	best before ...
Spezialitäten	specialities

hier ist jeden Tag bis 13 Uhr Markt
there's a market here every day until 1pm

an der Ecke ist ein Lebensmittelgeschäft, das lange offen hat
there's a grocer's on the corner that's open late

CLOTHES

Expressing yourself

I'm looking for the menswear section
ich suche die Herrenabteilung
ish zooche dee hehrhen-apteylung

no thanks, I'm just looking
nein, danke, ich sehe mich nur um
neyn, danke, ish zaye mish noo-e um

can I try it on?
kann ich das anprobieren?
kan ish das anprhohbeeren?

the jacket doesn't fit
die Jacke passt nicht
dee yake past nisht

I'd like to try on the shirt in the window
ich würde gern das Hemd aus dem Schaufenster anprobieren
ish vuurde gehrn das hehmt ows daym showfehnste anprhohbeeren

do you have these in a 39? *(shoe size)*
ich hätte gern diese hier in neununddreißig
ish hehte gehrn deeze hee-e in noyn-unt-drhey-sish

where are the changing rooms?
wo sind die Umkleiden?
voh zint dee umkleyden?

the trousers are too big/small
die Hose ist zu groß/klein
dee hohze ist tsoo grhohs/kleyn

I'll think about it
ich überlege es mir
ish uube-layge ehs mee-e

do you have it in another colour?
haben Sie das in einer anderen Farbe?
haaben zee das in eyne anderhen faabe?

do you have it in a smaller/bigger size?
haben Sie das in einer kleineren/größeren Größe?
haaben zee das in eyne kleynerhen/grheuserhen grheuse?

do you have the blouse in red?
haben Sie die Bluse auch in Rot?
haaben zee dee blooze owch in rhoht?

yes, that's fine, I'll take it
ja, danke, ich nehme das
yaa, danke, ish nayme das

no, I don't like it
nein, das gefällt mir nicht
neyn, das gefehlt mee-e nisht

I'd like to exchange this shirt, it doesn't fit
ich möchte dieses Hemd umtauschen, es passt nicht
ish meushte deezes hehmt umtowshen, ehs past nisht

the coat has a hole in it, can I get a refund?
der Mantel hat ein Loch, kann ich ihn zurückgeben?
daye mantel hat eyn loch, kan ish een tsoorhuuk-gayben?

Understanding

Damenbekleidung	ladieswear
Herrenbekleidung	menswear
Kinderbekleidung	children's clothes
reduzierte Ware ist vom Umtausch ausgeschlossen	sale items cannot be returned
Umkleide	changing rooms
Wäsche	lingerie

guten Tag, kann ich Ihnen helfen?
hello, can I help you?

wir haben ihn/sie/es nur in Blau und Schwarz
we only have it in blue or black

in dieser Größe haben wir nichts mehr da
we don't have any left in that size

steht Ihnen gut
it suits you

er/sie/es sitzt gut
it's a good fit

Sie können ihn/sie/es zurückbringen, wenn er/sie/es nicht passt
you can bring it back if it doesn't fit

SOUVENIRS AND PRESENTS

Expressing yourself

I'm looking for a present to take home
ich suche ein Mitbringsel
ish zooche eyn mitbrhingzel

I'd like something that's easy to transport
ich möchte etwas, das leicht zu transportieren ist
ish meushte ehtvas, das leysht tsoo trhansporteeren ist

it's for a little girl of four
es ist für ein vierjähriges Mädchen
ehs ist fuu-e eyn fee-e-yehrhiges mehtshen

could you gift-wrap it for me?
können sie es mir als Geschenk einpacken?
keunen zee ehs mee-e als geshehnk eynpaken?

Understanding

aus Holz/Silber/Gold/Wolle	made of wood/silver/gold/wool
Handarbeit	handmade
traditionelle Herstellung	traditionally made product

wie viel möchten Sie ausgeben?
how much do you want to spend?

soll es ein Geschenk sein?
is it a present?

das ist typisch für die Gegend
it's typical of the region

PHOTOS

The basics

black-and-white film	der Schwarzweißfilm *daye shvaats-veys-film*
camera	die Kamera *dee kamerha*
colour film	der Farbfilm *daye faabfilm*
copy	der Abzug *daye aptsook*
digital camera	die Digitalkamera *dee digitaal-kamerha*
disposable camera	die Einmal-Kamera *dee eynmaal-kamerha*
exposure	die Belichtung *dee belishtung*; (duration) die Belichtungszeit *dee belishtungs-tseyt*
film	der Film *daye film*
flash	der Blitz *daye blits*
glossy	glänzend *glehntsent*
matt	matt *mat*
memory card	die Speicherkarte *dee shpeyshe-kaate*
negative	das Negativ *das naygateef*
passport photo	das Passbild *das pasbilt*
photo booth	der Passbildautomat *daye pasbilt-owtohmaat*
reprint	der Abzug *daye aptsook*
slide	das Dia *das dee-a*
to get photos developed	Fotos entwickeln lassen *fohtohs ehntvikeln lasen*
to take a photo/ photos	ein Foto/Fotos machen *eyn fohtoh/fohtohs machen*

Expressing yourself

could you take a photo of us, please?
könnten Sie bitte ein Foto von uns machen?
keunten zee bite eyn fohtoh fon uns machen?

you just have to press this button
Sie müssen einfach auf diesen Knopf drücken
zee muusen eynfach owf deezen knopf drhuuken

I'd like a 200-ASA colour film
ich möchte einen 200-ASA-Farbfilm
ish meushte eynen tsvey-hundert aasaa faabfilm

do you have black-and-white films?
haben Sie Schwarzweißfilme?
haaben zee shvaats-veys-filme?

how much is it to develop a film of 36 photos?
wie viel kostet die Entwicklung eines Sechsunddreißigerfilms?
vee feel kostet dee ehntviklung eynes zehks-unt-drheysige-films?

I'd like to have this film developed
ich möchte diesen Film entwickeln lassen
ish meushte deezen film ehntvikeln lasen

I'd like extra copies of some of the photos
ich möchte von einigen Fotos mehrere Abzüge
ish meushte fon eynigen fohtohs mayrherhe aptsuuge

three copies of this one and two of this one
drei Abzüge von diesem und zwei von diesem
drhey aptsuuge fon deezem unt tsvey fon deezem

can I print my digital photos here?
kann ich hier Digitalfotos machen lassen?
kan ish hee-e digitaal-fohtohs machen lasen?

can you put these photos on a CD for me?
können Sie diese Fotos für mich auf CD speichern?
keunen zee deeze fohtohs fuu-e mish owf tsay-day shpeyshern?

I've come to pick up my photos
ich möchte meine Fotos abholen
ish meushte meyne fohtohs aphohlen

I've got a problem with my camera
ich habe ein Problem mit meiner Kamera
ish haabe eyn prhohblaym mit meyne kamerha

I don't know what's wrong with it
ich weiß nicht, was damit los ist
ish veys nisht, vas damit lohs ist

the flash doesn't work
der Blitz funktioniert nicht
daye blits funktsiohneert nisht

do you sell memory cards?
haben Sie Speicherkarten?
haaben zee shpeyshe-kaaten?

Understanding

Digitalbilder auf Fotopapier	digital pictures on photographic paper
Digitalfotos von CDs und Speicherkarten	digital photos from CDs and memory cards
Farbbilder sofort/über Nacht	colour photos developed while you wait/overnight
in einer Stunde	in one hour
Nachtexpress	overnight developing
Passbilder	passport photos

vielleicht ist die Batterie leer
maybe the battery's dead

wie ist Ihr Name?
what's the name, please?

wann brauchen Sie die Fotos?
when do you want the photos for?

wir können sie in einer Stunde entwickeln
we can develop them in an hour

Ihre Fotos sind am Donnerstag um 12 Uhr fertig
your photos will be ready at twelve o'clock on Thursday

PHOTOS

BANKS

Banks are usually open from 8.30am to 4 or 5pm, Monday to Friday, although some are closed for lunch. Cash machines often display a blue **EC** logo. You should be aware that some shops do not accept card payments, either by debit or credit card.

The basics

bank account	das Bankkonto *das bank-kontoh*
bank	die Bank *dee bank*
banknote	der Schein *daye sheyn*
bureau de change	die Wechselstube *dee **vehk**sel-shtoobe*
cash	das Bargeld *das **baa**gehlt* >>bn-as: added
cash machine	der Geldautomat *daye **gehlt**-owtohmaat*
change	das Wechselgeld *das **vehk**sel-gehlt*
cheque	der Scheck *daye shehk*
coin	die Münze *dee **muun**tse*
commission	die Provision *dee prhohvi**ziohn***
credit card	die Kreditkarte *dee krhehd**eet**kaate*
PIN (number)	die PIN *dee pin*
transfer	die Überweisung *dee **uube**veyzung*
traveller's cheque	der Reisescheck *daye **rhey**ze-shehk*
withdrawal	die Abhebung *dee **ap**haybung*
to change	wechseln **vehk**seln
to withdraw	abheben **ap**hayben

Expressing yourself

where I can get some money changed?
wo kann ich Geld wechseln?
*voh kan ish gehlt **vehk**seln?*

what time does the bank close?
bis wann hat die Bank geöffnet?
*bis van hat dee bank ge-**euf**net?*

I'm looking for a cash machine
ich suche einen Geldautomaten
ish zooche eynen gehlt-owtohmaaten

I'd like to change £100
ich möchte gerne 100 Pfund wechseln
ish meushte gehrne hundert pfunt vehkseln

what commission do you charge?
wie hoch ist die Provision?
vee hohch ist dee prhohviziohn?

I'd like to transfer some money
ich möchte Geld überweisen
ish meushte gehlt uubeveyzen

I'd like to report the loss of my credit card
ich möchte den Verlust meiner Kreditkarte melden
ish meushte dayn fehrlust meyne krhehdeetkaate mehlden

the cash machine has swallowed my card
der Geldautomat hat meine Karte eingezogen
daye gehlt-owtohmaat hat meyne kaate eyn-getsohgen

Understanding

Bitte geben Sie Ihre Karte ein
please insert your card

Bitte geben Sie Ihre PIN ein
please enter your PIN number

Bitte wählen Sie den gewünschten Betrag
please select the amount you require

Bitte entnehmen Sie Ihre Karte
please remove your card

außer Betrieb
out of service

POST OFFICES

Post offices and postboxes are identifiable by a yellow sign featuring a black horn. Post offices are generally open from 9am to 6pm Monday to Friday, and from 9am to midday on Saturdays. In large railway stations and at airports, post offices may stay open later and some are open on Sundays. There are sometimes post office counters in underground stations and some stationery shops. Post offices also sell envelopes and other items of stationery. A stamp for a postcard sent within Germany or the EU (as well as to Turkey and Switzerland) costs 45 cents and one to other countries 1 euro. Domestic mail is usually delivered the next day, but items posted abroad take three to six days to arrive. Stamps are usually only sold in post offices, although some tourist shops provide them with postcards. Postboxes with Sunday collections are marked with a red dot.

The basics

airmail	die Luftpost dee *luft*post
envelope	der Umschlag *daye um*shlaak
letter	der Brief *daye* brheef
mail	die Post dee post
parcel	*(small)* das Päckchen das *pehk*shen; *(big)* das Paket das pa*kayt*
post	die Post dee post
postbox	der Briefkasten *daye* brheef*kasten*
postcard	die Postkarte dee post*kaate*
postcode	die Postleitzahl dee post*leyt*-tsaal
post office	die Post dee post
stamp	die Briefmarke dee brheef*maake*
to mail, to post	*(send)* abschicken *ap*shiken; *(put in postbox)* einwerfen eyn*vehrfen*
to send	schicken *shiken*
to write	schreiben *shrhey*ben

Expressing yourself

is there a post office around here?
ist hier in der Nähe eine Post?
*ist hee-e in daye <u>neh</u>e **ey**ne post?*

is there a postbox near here?
ist hier in der Nähe ein Briefkasten?
*ist hee-e in daye <u>neh</u>e eyn **brheef**kasten?*

what time does the post office open?
wann öffnet die Post?
*van **euf**net die post?*

what time does the post office close?
wann schließt die Post?
van shleest die post?

do you sell stamps?
haben Sie Briefmarken?
*ha**a**ben zee **brheef**maaken?*

I'd like ... stamps for the UK, please
ich möchte bitte ... Briefmarken für Großbritannien
*ish **meush**te **bit**e ... **brheef**maaken <u>fuu</u>-e grhohs-brhi**tan**ien*

how long will the postcard/the letter/the parcel take to arrive?
wie lange braucht die Postkarte/der Brief/das Paket?
*vee **lang**e brhowcht dee **post**kaate/daye brheef/das pa**kayt**?*

where can I buy envelopes?
wo kann ich Umschläge kaufen?
*voh kan ish **um**sh<u>leh</u>ge **kow**fen?*

is there any post for me?
ist Post für mich gekommen?
*ist post <u>fuu</u>-e mish ge**ko**men?*

Understanding

Absender	sender
Nachtleerung	late-evening collection
Spätleerung	early-evening collection
Tagesleerungen	collections during the day
Vorsicht, zerbrechlich!	handle with care

er/sie/es braucht drei bis fünf Tage
it'll take between three and five days

der Brief/das Paket hat Übergewicht und kostet deshalb ...
the letter's/the parcel's overweight, which means it'll cost ...

INTERNET CAFÉS AND E-MAIL

Internet cafés are mainly found in big cities. If you bring your laptop, remember to bring adaptors for the mains and phone sockets (although you can buy these in specialist shops in Germany). Note that the German keyboard is slightly different from the "QWERTY" one you may be used to.

The basics

at-sign	das at-Zeichen *das at-tseyshen*
e-mail	die E-Mail *dee eemayl*
e-mail address	die E-Mail-Adresse *dee eemayl-adrhehse*
Internet café	das Internetcafé *das internehtkafay*
key	die Taste *dee taste*
keyboard	die Tastatur *dee tastatoo-e*
mouse	die Maus *dee mows*
password	das Passwort *das pasvort*
to click on	klicken auf *kliken owf*
to download	herunterladen *hehrhunte-laaden*
to e-mail	mailen *maylen*
to send an e-mail	eine E-Mail verschicken *eyne eemayl fehrshiken*

Expressing yourself

is there an Internet café near here?
ist hier in der Nähe ein Internetcafé?
ist hee-e in daye nehe eyn internehtkafay?

do you have an e-mail address?
haben Sie eine E-Mail-Adresse?
haaben zee eyne eemayl-adrhehse?

my e-mail address is john.brown@network.com
meine E-Mail-Adresse ist john.brown@network.com
meyne eemayl-adrhehse ist john punkt brown at network punkt com

I'd just like to check my e-mails
ich möchte nur schnell meine E-Mails lesen
ish meushte noo-e shnehl meyne eemayls layzen

would you mind helping me, I'm not sure what to do
könnten Sie mir bitte helfen, ich weiß nicht, wie es geht
keunten zee mee-e bite hehlfen, ish veys nisht, vee ehs gayt

I can't find the at-sign on this keyboard
ich finde das at-Zeichen auf dieser Tastatur nicht
ish finde das at-tseyshen owf deeze tastatoo-e nisht

it's not working
es funktioniert nicht
ehs funktsiohneert nisht

the computer's crashed
der Computer ist abgestürzt
daye kompyoote ist apgeshtuurtst

how much will it be for half an hour?
wie viel kostet eine halbe Stunde?
vee feel kostet eyne halbe shtunde?

how do I get online?
wie komme ich ins Internet?
vee kome ish ins interneht?

when do I pay?
wann muss ich bezahlen?
van mus ish betsaalen?

Understanding

Adressbuch	Address Book
Antworten	Reply
Ausschneiden	Cut
Drucken	Print
Einfügen	Paste; Attach
Empfangen	Receive
Kopieren	Copy
Löschen	Delete
Neue E-Mail	New Mail
Postausgang	Outbox
Posteingang	Inbox
Speichern	Save
Suchen	Find
Weiterleiten	Forward

Sie müssen etwa zwanzig Minuten warten
you'll have to wait for 20 minutes or so

fragen Sie ruhig, wenn Sie Hilfe brauchen
just ask if you're not sure what to do

Sie müssen dieses Passwort eingeben
just enter this password

TELEPHONE

Few phone boxes take coins these days. You can buy 5-euro or 10-euro phonecards in Telekom shops (indicated by a pink T), at most post offices and at some kiosks.

When giving their phone numbers, Germans read out every digit separately. 0 is pronounced **null** and 2 can be either **zwei** or **zwo** (to help distinguish it from **drei**). For example, 06151 772081 would be read as **null, sechs, eins, fünf, eins, sieben, sieben, zwei** (or **zwo**), **null, acht, eins**. When making or receiving a call, you should always say your name first. When you hang up, remember not to say **auf Wiedersehen** but **auf Wiederhören** (**sehen** = see, **hören** = hear).

To call the UK from Germany, first dial 00 44 and then the full phone number, minus the first 0 of the area code. To call Germany from the UK, dial 00 49 and then the full phone number, minus the first 0 of the area code. To call one German town from another, dial the whole number, including the first 0 of the area code.

Calls made to numbers beginning with 0800 are free. Those made to numbers beginning with 0180 are cheaper than normal, while 0190 numbers are particularly expensive.

See the chapter Useful Addresses and Phone Numbers for information about directory enquiries.

The basics

answering machine	der Anrufbeantworter *daye anrhoof-beantvorte*
call	der Anruf *daye anrhoof*
directory enquiries	die Auskunft *dee owskunft*
hello	hallo *haloh*
international call	das Auslandsgespräch *das owslants-geshprhehsh*
local call	das Ortsgespräch *das orts-geshprhehsh*
mailbox	die Mailbox *dee maylboks*

message	die Nachricht *dee nachrhisht*
mobile	das Handy *das hehndee*
national call	das Ferngespräch *das fehrn-geshprhehsh*
phone	das Telefon *das taylehfohn*
phone book	das Telefonbuch *das taylehfohn-booch*
phone box	die Telefonzelle *dee taylehfohn-tsehle*
phone number	die Telefonnummer *dee taylehfohn-nume*
phonecard	die Telefonkarte *dee taylehfohn-kaate*
text (message)	die SMS *dee ehs-ehm-ehs*
top-up card	die Guthabenkarte *dee goothaaben-kaate*
Yellow Pages®	die gelben Seiten *dee gehlben zeyten*
to call	anrufen *anrhoofen*
to phone	anrufen *anrhoofen*

Expressing yourself

where can I buy a phonecard?
wo kann ich eine Telefonkarte kaufen?
voh kan ish eyne taylehfohn-kaate kowfen?

a ...-euro top-up card, please
eine Guthabenkarte für ... Euro bitte
eyne goothaaben-kaate fuu-e ... oyrhoh bite

I'd like to make a reverse-charge call
ich möchte ein R-Gespräch führen
ish meushte eyn ehrh-geshprhehsh fuurhen

is there a phone box near here?
ist hier in der Nähe eine Telefonzelle?
ist hee-e in daye nehe eyne taylehfohn-tsehle?

can I recharge my phone here?
kann ich mein Handy hier aufladen?
kan ish meyn hehndee hee-e owflaaden?

do you have a mobile number?
sind Sie mobil zu erreichen?
zint zee mohbeel tsoo ehrheyshen?

where can I contact you?
wie kann ich Sie erreichen?
vee kan ish zee ehrheyshen?

did you get my message?
haben Sie meine Nachricht erhalten?
haaben zee meyne nachrhisht ehrhalten?

I'll text you
ich schicke Ihnen eine SMS
ish shike eenen eyne ehs-ehm-ehs

please text me
bitte schicken Sie mir eine SMS
bite shiken zee mee-e eyne ehs-ehm-ehs

Understanding

kein Anschluss unter dieser Nummer
the number you have dialled has not been recognized

bitte warten Sie
please hold the line

MAKING A CALL

Expressing yourself

hello, this is David Brown (speaking)
hallo, hier ist David Brown
haloh, hee-e ist David Brown

hello, could I speak to ..., please?
hallo, könnte ich bitte ... sprechen?
haloh, keunte ish bite ... shprhehshen?

hello, is that Manfred Berger?
hallo, spreche ich mit Manfred Berger?
haloh, shprhehshe ish mit manfrhayt behrge?

do you speak English?
sprechen Sie Englisch?
shprhehshen zee ehnglish?

could you speak more slowly, please?
könnten Sie bitte langsamer sprechen?
keunten zee bite langzaame shprhehshen?

I can't hear you, could you speak up, please?
ich verstehe Sie nicht, könnten Sie bitte lauter sprechen?
ish fehrstaye zee nisht, keunten zee bite lowte shprhehshen?

could you tell him/her I called?
könnten Sie ihm/ihr bitte sagen, dass ich angerufen habe?
keunten zee eem/ee-e bite zaagen, das ish angerhoofen haabe?

could you ask him/her to call me back?
könnten Sie ihm/ihr bitte sagen, dass er/sie mich zurückrufen soll?
keunten zee eem/ee-e bite zaagen, das aye/zee mish tsoorhuuk-rhoofen zol?

my name is ... and my number is ...
mein Name ist ... und meine Nummer ist ...
meyn naame ist ... unt meyne nume ist ...

do you know when he/she might be available?
wissen Sie, wann ich ihn/sie erreichen kann?
visen zee, van ish een/zee ehrheyshen kan?

I'll call back later
ich rufe später noch einmal an
ish rhoofe shpehte noch eynmaal an

thank you, goodbye
vielen Dank, auf Wiederhören
feelen dank, owf veede-heurhen

Understanding

wer ist da bitte?
who's calling?

Sie haben sich verwählt
you've got the wrong number

er ist gerade nicht da
he's not here at the moment

soll ich etwas ausrichten?
do you want to leave a message?

ich sage ihr, dass Sie angerufen haben
I'll tell her you called

ich sage ihm, dass er Sie zurückrufen soll
I'll ask him to call you back

bleiben Sie bitte am Apparat
please hold the line

ich gebe sie Ihnen
I'll hand you over to her

einen Augenblick bitte, ich verbinde Sie
one moment please, I'll put you through

PROBLEMS

Expressing yourself

I don't know the code
ich weiß die Vorwahl nicht
*ish veys dee **fohe**-vaal nisht*

it's engaged
es ist besetzt
*ehs ist be**zehtst***

there's no reply
es nimmt niemand ab
*ehs nimt **nee**mant ap*

I couldn't get through
ich bin nicht durchgekommen
*ish bin nisht **dursh**-gekomen*

we're about to get cut off
das Gespräch bricht gleich ab
*das ge**shprhehsh** brhisht gleysh ap*

the reception's really bad
der Empfang ist sehr schlecht
*daye ehm**pfang** ist zaye shlehsht*

I don't have much credit left on my phone
mein Guthaben ist fast alle
*meyn **goot**haaben ist fast **al**e*

I can't get a signal
ich habe keinen Empfang
*ish **haa**be **key**nen ehm**pfang***

Understanding

ich höre Sie kaum
I can hardly hear you

die Verbindung ist schlecht
it's a bad line

Common abbreviations

dienstl. = dienstlich work (number)
mobil = Mobiltelefonnummer mobile (number)
priv. = privat home (number)
Tel.-Nr. = Telefonnummer phone number

HEALTH

If you are an EU national, you should have or apply for a European Health Insurance Card (which has replaced the old E111 form) to cover you for any medical treatment you may need in Germany. You may have to pay some of the cost and then claim a refund. Be sure to keep all relevant documents, including receipts and prescriptions.

Pharmacies (**Apotheke**) have the same opening hours as other shops. The address and opening times of the nearest out-of-hours pharmacist are displayed in the window. Pharmacies are the only places where you can buy medicines, even non-prescription drugs.

Doctors' addresses can usually be found at your accommodation, or consult the **Ärzte** (doctors) section of the Yellow Pages® under the heading **Gesundheitswesen**. Doctors' surgeries are usually open from 10am to midday, and from 4 to 6pm, except on Wednesdays and at weekends. In a medical emergency, dial 112.

The basics

allergy	die Allergie *dee alehrgee*
ambulance	der Krankenwagen *daye krhanken-vaagen*
aspirin	die Kopfschmerztablette *dee kopf-shmehrts-tablehte*
blood	das Blut *das bloot*
broken	gebrochen *gebrhochen*
casualty (department)	die Unfallstation *dee unfal-shtatsiohn*
chemist's	die Apotheke *dee apohtayke*
condom	das Kondom *das kondohm*
dentist	der Zahnarzt *daye tsaan-aatst*
diarrhoea	der Durchfall *daye durshfal*
doctor	der Arzt *daye aatst*
food poisoning	die Lebensmittelvergiftung *dee laybens-mitel-fehrgiftung*
GP	der Allgemeinarzt *daye algemeyn-aatst*

gynaecologist	der Frauenarzt *daye frhowen-aatst*
hospital	das Krankenhaus *das krhankenhows*
infection	die Infektion *dee infehktsiohn*
injury	die Verletzung *dee fehrletsung*
medicine	das Medikament *das mehdikamehnt*
painkiller	das Schmerzmittel *das shmehrts-mitel*
period	(menstruation) die Periode *dee pehrhiohde*
plaster	(for a cut) das Pflaster *das pflaste*
rash	der Ausschlag *daye ows-shlaak*
sunburn	der Sonnenbrand *daye zonenbrhant*
surgical spirit	der Alkohol *daye alkoh-hohl*
tablet	die Tablette *dee tablehte*
temperature	das Fieber *das feebe*
vaccination	die Impfung *dee impfung*
X-ray	das Röntgen *das rheuntgen*
to disinfect	desinfizieren *dehsinfitseerehn*
to faint	ohnmächtig werden *ohnmehshtish vehrden*
to vomit	sich erbrechen *zish ehrbrhehshen*
to X-ray	röntgen *rheuntgen*

Expressing yourself

does anyone have an aspirin/a tampon/a plaster, by any chance?
hat jemand zufällig eine Kopfschmerztablette/einen Tampon/ein Pflaster?
hat yaymant tsoofehlish eyne kopf-shmehrts-tablehte/eynen tampon/eyn pflaste?

I need to see a doctor
ich muss zum Arzt
ish mus tsum aatst

where can I find a doctor?
wo finde ich einen Arzt?
voh finde ish eynen aatst?

I'd like to make an appointment for today
ich hätte gern einen Termin für heute
ish hehte gehrn eynen tehrmeen fuu-e hoyte

as soon as possible
so bald wie möglich
zoh balt vee meuglish

can you send an ambulance?
können Sie einen Krankenwagen schicken?
keunen zee eynen krhanken-vaagen shiken?

I've broken my glasses
meine Brille ist kaputt
meyne brhile ist kaput

I've lost a contact lens
ich habe eine Kontaktlinse verloren
ish haabe eyne kontaktlinze fehrlohrhen

Arztpraxis   doctor's surgery
Notaufnahme   casualty department
Rezept   prescription

bis Dienstag gibt es keine Termine
there are no available appointments until Thursday

geht es am Freitag um 14 Uhr?
is Friday at 2pm all right?

wie ist Ihr Name und ihre Adresse?
what's your name and address?

AT THE DOCTOR'S OR THE HOSPITAL

Expressing yourself

I have an appointment with Dr ...
ich habe einen Termin bei Dr. ...
ish haabe eynen tehrmeen bey doktohe ...

I've been stung/bitten by ...
ich bin von ... gestochen/gebissen worden
ish bin fon ... geshtochen/gebisen vorden

I feel very weak
ich fühle mich sehr schwach
ish fuule mish zaye shvach

I don't know what it is
ich weiß nicht, was es ist
ish veis nisht, vas ehs ist

I've got a headache
ich habe Kopfschmerzen
ish haabe kopf-shmehrtsen

I've got a sore throat
ich habe Halsschmerzen
ish haabe hals-shmehrtsen

I've got toothache/stomachache
ich habe Zahnschmerzen/Magenschmerzen
ish haabe tsaan-shmehrtsen/maagen-shmehrtsen

my back hurts
ich habe Rückenschmerzen
ish haabe rhuuken-shmehrtsen

it hurts (here)
es tut (hier) weh
ehs toot (hee-e) vay

it's got worse
es ist schlimmer geworden
ehs ist shlime gevorden

it started last night
es hat letzte Nacht angefangen
ehs hat lehtste nacht angefangen

I have asthma
ich habe Asthma
ish haabe astma

it itches
es juckt
ehs yukt

I've got diarrhoea
ich habe Durchfall
ish haabe durshfal

I feel sick
mir ist schlecht
mee-e ist shlehsht

for three days
seit drei Tagen
zeyt drhey taagen

I've got a temperature
ich habe Fieber
ish haabe feebe

I have a heart condition
ich bin herzkrank
ish bin hehrts-krhank

I'm on the pill/the minipill
ich nehme die Pille/die Minipille
ish nayme dee pile/dee minipile

I'm four months pregnant
ich bin im vierten Monat schwanger
ish bin im fee-eten mohnat shvange

I'm allergic to penicillin
ich bin allergisch gegen Penizillin
ish bin allehrgish gaygen pehnitsileen

I've twisted my ankle
ich habe mir den Knöchel verstaucht
ish haabe mee-e dayn kneushel fehrshtowcht

I fell and hurt my back
ich bin hingefallen und habe mich am Rücken verletzt
ish bin hingefalen unt haabe mish am rhuuken fehrletst

HEALTH

it's never happened to me before
ich hatte das noch nie
ish hate das noch nee

I've been on antibiotics for a week and I'm not getting any better
ich nehme seit einer Woche Antibiotika, aber es wird nicht besser
ish nayme zeyt eyne voche antibiohtikaa, aabe ehs virt nisht behse

I can't eat anything without vomiting
ich kann nichts essen, ohne mich zu übergeben
ish kan nishts ehsen ohne mish tsoo uubegayben

I've lost a filling
mir ist eine Füllung herausgefallen
mee-e ist eyne fuulung hehrows-gefalen

how is he/she?
wie geht es ihm/ihr?
vee gayt ehs eem/ee-e?

I've had a blackout
ich bin ohnmächtig geworden
ish bin ohnmehshtish gevorden

is it serious?
ist es schlimm?
ist ehs shlim?

is it contagious?
ist es ansteckend?
ist ehs anshtehkent?

how much do I owe you?
was schulde ich Ihnen?
vas shulde ish eenen?

can I have a receipt?
kann ich bitte eine Rechnung haben?
kan ish bite eyne rhehshnung haaben?

Understanding

bitte nehmen Sie im Wartezimmer Platz
if you'd like to take a seat in the waiting room

wo tut es weh?
where does it hurt?

atmen Sie tief ein
take a deep breath

legen Sie sich bitte hin
lie down, please

machen Sie bitte den Oberkörper frei
can you take off your shirt/blouse, please?

tut es weh, wenn ich hier drücke?
does it hurt when I press here?

sind Sie gegen ... geimpft?
have you been vaccinated against …?

sind Sie allergisch gegen ...?
are you allergic to …?

nehmen Sie irgendwelche anderen Medikamente?
are you taking any other medication?

ich stelle Ihnen ein Rezept aus
I'll write you a prescription

in ein paar Tagen müsste es Ihnen wieder besser gehen
it should clear up in a few days

kommen Sie in einer Woche noch einmal vorbei
come back and see me in a week

Sie müssen operiert werden   **Sie sollten sich schonen**
you're going to need an operation   you should take things easy

HEALTH

AT THE CHEMIST'S

Expressing yourself

I'd like a box of plasters, please
ich möchte eine Packung Pflaster bitte
ish meushte eyne pakung pflaste bite

could I have something for a bad cold?
ich brauche etwas gegen eine schwere Erkältung
ish brhowche ehtvas gaygen eyne shvayrhe ehrkehltung

I need something for a cough
ich brauche etwas gegen Husten
ish brhowche ehtvas gaygen hoosten

I'm allergic to aspirin
ich bin allergisch gegen Acetylsalicylsäure
ish bin allehrgish gaygen atsehtuul-zalitsuul-zoyrhe

I need the morning-after pill
ich brauche die Pille danach
ish brhowche dee pile danach

I'd like to try a homeopathic remedy
ich hätte gern ein homöopathisches Mittel
ish hehte gehrn eyn hohmeu-ohpaatishes mitel

I'd like a bottle of solution for soft contact lenses
ich brauche eine Lösung für weiche Kontaktlinsen
ish brhowche eyne leuzung fuu-e veyshe kontaktlinzen

Understanding

Creme	cream
dreimal täglich vor dem Essen einnehmen	take three times a day before meals
Gegenanzeigen	contraindications
Kapseln	capsules
Nebenwirkungen	possible side effects
Puder	powder
rezeptpflichtig	available on prescription only
Salbe	ointment
Tabletten	tablets
Tropfen	drops
Zäpfchen	suppositories
zum Auftragen auf ...	to be applied to ...
zum Einnehmen	for internal use

HEALTH

Some informal expressions

ich bin nicht auf dem Damm I'm not feeling 100 percent
mir dreht sich alles my head's spinning

PROBLEMS AND EMERGENCIES

The police in Germany can be identified by their green uniforms and green cars marked **Polizei**. They are well-trained and most speak English. They are usually happy to help tourists.

A lost property office is called a **Fundbüro**.

In an emergency, dial 110 for the police and 112 for the fire brigade or an ambulance. You should be ready to produce your passport or other form of ID.

The basics

accident	der Unfall *daye unfal*
ambulance	der Krankenwagen *daye krhankenvaagen*
broken	(limb, bone) gebrochen *gebrhochen*
coastguard	die Küstenwacht *dee kuustenvacht*
disabled	behindert *behindert*
doctor	der Arzt *daye aatst*
emergency	der Notfall *daye nohtfal*
fire	das Feuer *das foye*
fire brigade	die Feuerwehr *dee foyerwaye*
hospital	das Krankenhaus *das krhankenhows*
ill	krank *krhank*
injured	verletzt *fehrletst*
police	die Polizei *dee politsey*

Expressing yourself

can you help me?
können Sie mir helfen?
keunen see mee-e hehlfen?

help!
Hilfe!
hilfe!

fire!
Feuer!
foye!

be careful!
Achtung!
achtung!

it's an emergency!
es ist ein Notfall!
ehs ist eyn nohtfal!

could I use your phone, please?
kann ich mal telefonieren?
kan ish maal taylehfohneeren?

there's been an accident
es ist ein Unfall passiert
ehs ist eyn unfal paseert

does anyone here speak English?
spricht hier irgendjemand Englisch?
shprhisht hee-e irgent-yaymant ehnglish?

I need to contact the British consulate
ich muss mich mit dem britischen Konsulat in Verbindung setzen
ish mus mish mit daym brhitishen konzoolaat in fehrbindung zehtsen

where's the nearest police station?
wo ist das nächste Polizeirevier?
voh ist das nehkste politsey-rhevee-e?

what do I have to do?
was soll ich tun?
vas zol ish toon?

my bag's been snatched
meine Tasche ist gestohlen worden
meyne tashe ist geshtohlen vorden

I've lost …
ich habe … verloren
ish haabe … fehrlohrhen

I've been attacked
ich bin überfallen worden
ish bin uuberfalen vorden

I've broken down
ich habe eine Panne
ish haabe eyne pane

my car's been broken into
mein Auto ist aufgebrochen worden
meyn owtoh ist owfgebrhochen vorden

my passport/credit card has been stolen
mein Pass/meine Kreditkarte ist gestohlen worden
meyn pas/meyne krhehdeetkaate ist geshtohlen vorden

my son/daughter is missing
mein Sohn/meine Tochter ist verschwunden
meyn zohn/meyne tochte ist fehrshvunden

my car's been towed away
mein Auto ist abgeschleppt worden
meyn owtoh ist apgeshlehpt vorden

there's a man following me
ein Mann verfolgt mich
eyn man fehrfolgt mish

is there disabled access?
gibt es einen Behinderteneingang?
geept ehs eynen behinderten-eyngang?

can you keep an eye on my things for a minute?
können Sie einen Moment auf meine Sachen aufpassen?
keunen see eynen momehnt owf meyne zachen owfpasen?

he's drowning, get help!
er ertrinkt, holen Sie Hilfe!
aye ehrtrhinkt, hohlen zee hilfe!

Understanding

außer Betrieb	out of order
Bergwacht	mountain rescue
Feuerlöscher	fire extinguisher
Fundsachen	lost property
Notausgang	emergency exit
Notruf ...	in emergency call ...
Pannendienst	breakdown service
Vorsicht, bissiger Hund!	beware of the dog

POLICE

Expressing yourself

I want to report something stolen
ich möchte einen Diebstahl anzeigen
ish meushte eynen deep-shtaal an-tseygen

I need a document from the police for my insurance company
ich brauche eine polizeiliche Bestätigung für meine Versicherung
ish brhowche eyne politseylishe bestehtigung fuu-e meyne fehrzisherhung

Filling in forms	
Alter	age
Anschrift	address

Beruf	occupation
Familienname	surname
Geburtsdatum/Geburtstag	date of birth
Geburtsort	place of birth
Geschlecht	sex
Hausnummer	house number
Land	country
Passnummer	passport number
PLZ/Postleitzahl	postcode
Staatsangehörigkeit	nationality
Straße	street
Tag der Ankunft/Abreise	arrival/departure date
Telefonnummer	telephone number
Unterschrift	signature
Vorname	first name
Wohnort	town

für diese Ware müssen Sie Zoll bezahlen
there's customs duty to pay on this item

öffnen Sie bitte diese Tasche
would you open this bag, please?

was wurde gestohlen?
what's been stolen?

wann ist das passiert?
when did this happen?

wo wohnen Sie?
where are you staying?

können Sie ihn/sie/es beschreiben?
can you describe him/her/it?

bitte füllen Sie dieses Formular aus
would you fill in this form, please?

bitte unterschreiben Sie hier
would you sign here, please?

Some informal expressions

Bulle cop
einlochen to bang up
Knast clink

TIME AND DATE

The basics

after	nach *nach*
already	schon *shohn*
always	immer *ime*
at the moment	im Moment *im mohmehnt*
before	vor *fohe*
between ... and ...	zwischen ... und ... *tsvishen ... unt ...*
day	der Tag *daye taak*
during	während *vehrhent*
early	früh *frhuu*
evening	der Abend *daye aabent*
for a long time	lange *lange*
from ... to ...	von ... bis ... *fon ... bis ...*
from time to time	ab und zu *ap unt tsoo*
in a little while	in Kürze *in kuurtse*
last	letzte *lehtste*
late	spät *speht*
midday	der Mittag *daye mitaak*
midnight	die Mitternacht *dee mitenacht*
morning	der Morgen *daye morgen*
month	der Monat *daye mohnat*
never	nie *nee*
next	nächste *nehkste*
night	die Nacht *dee nacht*
not yet	noch nicht *noch nisht*
now	jetzt *yehtst*
occasionally	gelegentlich *gelaygentlish*
often	oft *oft*
rarely	selten *zehlten*
recently	vor kurzem *fohe kurtsem*
since	seit *zeyt*
sometimes	manchmal *manshmaal*
soon	bald *balt*
still	noch *noch*
straight away	sofort *zohfort*

until	bis *bis*
week	die Woche *dee vo*che
weekend	das Wochenende *das vo*chen-ehnde
year	das Jahr *das yaa*

Expressing yourself

see you soon!
bis bald!
bis balt!

see you later!
bis später!
bis spehte!

see you on Monday!
bis Montag!
bis mohntaak!

have a good weekend!
schönes Wochenende!
sheunes vochen-ehnde!

I haven't been there yet
ich war noch nicht dort
ish waa noch nisht dort

I haven't had time
ich hatte keine Zeit
ish hate keyne tseyt

I've got plenty of time
ich habe viel Zeit
ish haabe feel tseyt

I'm in a rush
ich bin in Eile
ish bin in eyle

hurry up!
Beeilung!
be-eylung!

just a minute, please
einen Moment bitte
eynen mohmehnt bite

I had a late night
gestern ist es spät geworden
gehstern ist ehs speht gevorden

I waited ages
ich habe ewig gewartet
ish haabe ayvish gevaatet

sorry I'm late
entschuldigen Sie die Verspätung
ehntshuldigen zee dee fehrspehtung

I have to get up very early tomorrow to catch my plane
ich muss morgen sehr früh aufstehen, um mein Flugzeug zu bekommen
ish mus morgen zaye frhuu owfstayen, um meyn floogtsoyk tsoo bekomen

we only have 4 days left
wir haben nur noch vier Tage
vee-e haaben noo-e noch fee-e taage

THE DATE

Giving the date

As in English, ordinal numbers are used for the date (first/second of January etc). German ordinal numbers (see the Numbers chapter) are written as the number followed by a full stop. For example, 2 January 2006 would be written 2. Januar 2006.

Note how the month, the year and the century are expressed differently in the following phrases:

in November	im November
on 17 May	am 17. (siebzehnten) Mai
I was born in 1970	ich bin 1970 geboren or ich bin im Jahre 1970 geboren
from 2005 to 2006	von 2005 bis 2006
between 2001 and 2006	zwischen 2001 und 2006
in the first century BC/AD	im 1. Jahrhundert vor Christus (v. Chr.)/nach Christus (n. Chr.)

The basics

... ago	vor ... *fohe ...*
at the beginning/end of	Anfang/Ende *anfang/ehn*de
in the middle of	Mitte *mit*e
in two days' time	in zwei Tagen *in tsvey taa*gen
last night	(evening) gestern Abend *gehs*tern *aa*bent; (night) gestern Nacht *gehs*tern nacht
the day after tomorrow	übermorgen *uu*be-morgen
the day before yesterday	vorgestern *fohe*-gehstern
today	heute *hoy*te
tomorrow	morgen *mor*gen
tomorrow morning/ afternoon/evening	morgen früh/Nachmittag/Abend *mor*gen *frhuu*/*nach*mitaak/*aa*bent

TIME AND DATE

yesterday	gestern *gehstern*
yesterday morning/	gestern Morgen/Nachmittag/Abend
afternoon/evening	*gehstern morgen/nachmitaak/aabent*

Expressing yourself

I was born in 1975
ich bin 1975 geboren
ish bin noyn-tsayn-hundert fuunf-unt-zeep-tsish gebohren

I came here a few years ago
ich bin vor ein paar Jahren hierhergekommen
ish bin fohe eyn paa yaarhen hee-e-hehrgekomen

I spent a month in Germany last summer
ich bin letzten Sommer einen Monat in Deutschland gewesen
ish bin lehtsten zome eynen mohnat in doytshlant gevayzen

I was here last year at the same time
letztes Jahr war ich um die gleiche Zeit hier
lehtstes yaa vaa ish um dee gleyshe tseyt hee-e

what's the date today?
der Wievielte ist heute?
daye veefeelte ist hoyte?

what day is it today?
was ist heute für ein Tag?
vas ist hoyte fuu-e eyn taak?

it's the 1st of May
es ist der erste Mai
ehs ist daye ayeste mey

I'm staying until Sunday
ich bleibe bis Sonntag
ish bleybe bis zontaak

we're leaving tomorrow
wir fahren morgen ab
vee-e faarhen morgen ap

I already have plans for Tuesday
ich habe am Dienstag schon etwas vor
ish haabe am deenstaak shohn ehtvas fohe

Understanding

dreimal in der Stunde/	three times an hour/a day/a
am Tag/im Monat	month
einmal/zweimal	once/twice

121

jeden Montag	every Monday
täglich	every day

es wurde Mitte des neunzehnten Jahrhunderts gebaut
it was built in the mid-nineteenth century

hier ist im Sommer sehr viel los
it gets very busy here in the summer

wann fahren Sie ab?	**wie lange bleiben Sie?**
when are you leaving?	how long are you staying?

THE TIME

Telling the time

Germans usually use the 24-hour clock to express the time of day. It is, however, also acceptable to say **morgens** (in the morning), **nachmittags** (in the afternoon) or **abends** (in the evening): 05.00 = fünf Uhr morgens, 17.00 = fünf Uhr nachmittags, 20.00 = acht Uhr abends.

Note that **halb** refers to half an hour before the indicated hour, and not after the hour as in English. Thus **halb drei** means half past two and not half past three.

Some informal expressions

Punkt 8 Uhr at 8 o'clock on the dot
Schlag Mitternacht on the stroke of midnight
um ganz/um halb on the hour/on the half-hour

The basics

a quarter of an hour	eine Viertelstunde *eyne firtel-shtunde*
at lunchtime	mittags *mitaaks*
at midnight	um Mitternacht *um mitenacht*

at night	nachts *nachts*
half an hour	eine halbe Stunde *eyne halbe shtunde*
in the afternoon	nachmittags *nachmitaaks*
in the evening	abends *aabents*
in the morning	morgens *morgens*
on time	pünktlich *puunktlish*
three quarters of an hour	eine Dreiviertelstunde *eyne drhey-firtel-shtunde*

Expressing yourself

excuse me, have you got the time, please?
entschuldigen Sie, können Sie mir bitte sagen, wie viel Uhr es ist?
ehntshuldigen zee, keunen zee mee-e bite zaagen, vee feel oo-e ehs ist?

it's exactly three o'clock
es ist genau drei Uhr
ehs ist genow dhrey oo-e

it's nearly one o'clock
es ist kurz vor eins
ehs ist kurts fohe eyns

it's ten past one
es ist zehn nach eins
ehs ist tsayn nach eyns

it's a quarter past one
es ist Viertel nach eins
ehs ist firtel nach eyns

it's a quarter to two
es ist Viertel vor zwei
ehs ist firtel fohe tsvey

it's twenty past twelve
es ist zwanzig nach zwölf
ehs ist tsvan-tsish nach tsveulf

it's twenty to five
es ist zwanzig vor fünf
ehs ist tsvan-tsish fohe fuunf

it's twenty-five past six
es ist fünf vor halb sieben
ehs ist fuunf fohe halp zeeben

it's half past one
es ist halb zwei
ehs ist halp tsvey

what time is it?
wie viel Uhr ist es?
vee feel oo-e ist ehs?

I arrived at about two o'clock
ich bin gegen zwei Uhr angekommen
ish bin gaygen tsvey oo-e angekomen

I set my alarm for nine
ich habe meinen Wecker auf neun gestellt
ish haabe meynen vehke owf noyn geshtehlt

I waited twenty minutes
ich habe zwanzig Minuten gewartet
ish haabe tsvan-tsish minooten gevaatet

the train was ten minutes late
der Zug hatte zehn Minuten Verspätung
daye tsook hate tsayn minooten fehrshpehtung

I got home an hour ago
ich bin vor einer Stunde nach Hause gekommen
ish bin fohe eyne shtunde nach howze gekomen

shall we meet in half an hour?
sollen wir uns in einer halben Stunde treffen?
zolen vee-e uns in eyne halben shtunde trhehfen?

I'll be back in a quarter of an hour
ich bin in einer Viertelstunde zurück
ish bin in eyne firtel-shtunde tsoorhuuk

there's a three-hour time difference between ... and ...
es sind drei Stunden Zeitunterschied zwischen ... und ...
ehs zint drhey shtunden tseyt-untesheet tsvishen ... unt ...

Understanding

von 10 bis 16 Uhr geöffnet
open from 10am to 4pm

es findet jeden Abend um sieben statt
it takes place every evening at seven

es dauert ungefähr eineinhalb Stunden
it lasts around an hour and a half

das Geschäft öffnet um zehn Uhr morgens
the shop opens at ten in the morning

der Bus fährt jede halbe Stunde
there's a bus every half-hour

NUMBERS

0	null	*nul*
1	eins	*eyns*
2	zwei	*tsvey*
3	drei	*drhey*
4	vier	*fee-e*
5	fünf	*fuunf*
6	sechs	*zehks*
7	sieben	*zeeben*
8	acht	*acht*
9	neun	*noyn*
10	zehn	*tsayn*
11	elf	*ehlf*
12	zwölf	*tsveulf*
13	dreizehn	*drhey-tsayn*
14	vierzehn	*fee-e-tsayn*
15	fünfzehn	*fuunf-tsayn*
16	sechzehn	*zehsh-tsayn*
17	siebzehn	*zeep-tsayn*
18	achtzehn	*ach-tsayn*
19	neunzehn	*noyn-tsayn*
20	zwanzig	*tsvan-tsish*
21	einundzwanzig	*eyn-unt-tsvan-tsish*
22	zweiundzwanzig	*tsvey-unt-tsvan-tsish*
30	dreißig	*drhey-sish*
35	fünfunddreißig	*fuunf-unt-drhey-sish*
40	vierzig	*fee-e-tsish*
50	fünfzig	*fuunf-tsish*
60	sechzig	*zehsh-tsish*
70	siebzig	*zeep-tsish*
80	achtzig	*ach-tsish*
90	neunzig	*noyn-tsish*
100	hundert	*hundert*
101	hunderteins	*hundert-eyns*
200	zweihundert	*tsvey-hundert*
500	fünfhundert	*fuunf-hundert*
1000	tausend	*towzent*
2000	zweitausend	*tsvey-towzent*

10000	zehntausend *tsayn-towzent*
1000000	eine Million *eyne miliohn*

first	erste *ayeste*
second	zweite *tsveyte*
third	dritte *drhite*
fourth	vierte *fee-ete*
fifth	fünfte *fuunfte*
sixth	sechste *zehkste*
seventh	siebte *zeepte*
eighth	achte *achte*
ninth	neunte *noynte*
tenth	zehnte *tsaynte*
twentieth	zwanzigste *tsvan-tsish-ste*

20 plus 3 equals 23
zwanzig plus drei ist dreiundzwanzig
tsvan-tsish plus drhey ist drhey-unt-tsvan-tsish

20 minus 3 equals 17
zwanzig minus drei ist siebzehn
tsvan-tsish meenus drhey ist zeep-tsayn

20 multiplied by 4 equals 80
zwanzig mal vier ist achtzig
tsvan-tsish maal fee-e ist ach-tsish

20 divided by 4 equals 5
zwanzig geteilt durch vier ist fünf
tsvan-tsish geteylt dursh fee-e ist fuunf

DICTIONARY

ENGLISH-GERMAN

A

a ein, eine
abbey die Abtei
able: to be able to können
about *(concerning)* über; *(before numbers, time etc)* ungefähr; **to be about to do** gerade tun wollen
above über
abroad im Ausland; *(go)* ins Ausland; **from abroad** aus dem Ausland
accept annehmen
access *(entrance)* der Eingang 116
accident der Unfall 31, 115
accommodation die Unterkunft
across *(to the other side of)* über; *(on the other side of)* auf der anderen Seite von; **across from** gegenüber von
adaptor der Adapter
address die Adresse 17
admission der Eintritt
advance: in advance vorher 67
advice der Rat; **to ask someone's advice** jemanden um Rat fragen
advise raten
after nach
afternoon der Nachmittag
after-sun (cream) die Après-Lotion
again noch einmal
against gegen
age das Alter
ago: ten years ago vor zehn Jahren
air die Luft
air conditioning die Klimaanlage
airline die Fluggesellschaft
airmail die Luftpost

airport der Flughafen
alarm clock der Wecker
alcohol der Alkohol
alive lebendig
all *(everything)* alles; *(everyone)* alle; **all day** den ganzen Tag; **all week** die ganze Woche; **all the better** umso besser; **all the same** trotzdem; **all the time** die ganze Zeit
allergic allergisch 112
almost fast
already schon
also auch
although obwohl
always immer
ambulance der Krankenwagen 109
America Amerika
American *(n)* der Amerikaner; *(female)* die Amerikanerin
American *(adj)* amerikanisch
among unter
anaesthetic die Narkose
and und
animal das Tier
ankle der Knöchel
another *(additional)* noch ein/eine; *(different)* ein anderer/eine andere/ein anderes
answer *(n)* die Antwort
answer *(v)* antworten
answering machine der Anrufbeantworter
ant die Ameise
antibiotics die Antibiotika
anybody, anyone *(everybody)* jeder; *(in questions)* jemand; *(in negative statements)* niemand

anything *(everything)* alles; *(in questions)* etwas; *(in negative statements)* nichts

anyway *(in any case)* sowieso; *(all the same)* trotzdem; *(to resume)* jedenfalls

apology die Entschuldigung

appendicitis die Blinddarmentzündung

appointment der Termin; **to make an appointment** einen Termin vereinbaren 108; **to have an appointment (with)** einen Termin haben (mit)

April April

area die Gegend; **in the area** in der Gegend

arm der Arm

around um ... herum; **around here/there** hier/dort in der Gegend; **be around** da sein

arrange *(put in order)* ordnen; *(plan)* planen; **to arrange to meet** sich verabreden

arrival die Ankunft

arrive ankommen

art die Kunst

artist der Künstler

as wie; *(when)* als; *(because)* weil; **as soon as possible** so bald wie möglich; **as soon as** sobald; **as well as** sowie

ashtray der Aschenbecher

ask fragen; **to ask a question** eine Frage stellen

aspirin die Kopfschmerztablette

asthma das Asthma

at *(town)* in; *(thing)* an; **at my father's** bei meinem Vater; **at one o'clock** um ein Uhr

attack überfallen 115

August August

autumn der Herbst

available verfügbar

avenue die Allee

away weg; **ten kilometres away** zehn Kilometer entfernt

ß

baby das Baby

baby's bottle die Babyflasche

back der Rücken; **at the back of the bus/book** hinten im Bus/Buch

backpack der Rucksack

bad schlecht

bag die Tasche

baggage das Gepäck

bake backen

baker's der Bäcker

balcony der Balkon

bandage der Verband

bank die Bank 94

banknote der Schein

bar die Bar

barbecue *(appliance)* der Grill; *(party)* die Grillparty

bath das Bad; *(tub)* die Badewanne; **to have a bath** baden

bathroom das Bad

bath towel das Badetuch

battery die Batterie 31

be sein

beach der Strand

beach umbrella der Sonnenschirm

beard der Bart

beautiful schön

because weil; **because of** wegen

bed das Bett

bee die Biene

before vor

begin anfangen

beginner der Anfänger

beginning der Anfang; **at the beginning** am Anfang

behind hinter

Belgian *(n)* der Belgier; *(female)* die Belgierin

Belgian *(adj)* belgisch

Belgium Belgien

believe glauben

below unter

beside neben

best beste; **the best** das Beste

better besser; **to get better** besser werden; **he's getting better** es geht ihm besser; **it's better to …** es ist besser, wenn …

between zwischen

bicycle das Fahrrad

bicycle pump die Luftpumpe

big groß

bike das Rad

bill die Rechnung **50**

bin der Abfalleimer

binoculars das Fernglas

birthday der Geburtstag

bit: a bit (of) ein bisschen

bite (n) der Biss

bite (v) beißen

black schwarz

blackout (fainting) der Ohnmachtsanfall; (power cut) der Stromausfall

blanket die Decke

bleed bluten

bless: bless you! Gesundheit!

blind blind

blister die Blase

blood das Blut

blood pressure der Blutdruck

blue blau

board das Brett; (at hotel) die Verpflegung

boat das Schiff

body der Körper

book (n) das Buch; **book of tickets** das Fahrkartenheft

book (v) reservieren; (ticket) vorbestellen

bookshop die Buchhandlung

boot der Stiefel; (of car) der Kofferraum

borrow ausleihen

botanical garden der botanische Garten

both beide; **both of us** wir beide

bottle die Flasche

bottle opener der Flaschenöffner

bottom (of glass, box etc) der Boden; **at the bottom** unten

bowl die Schüssel

boyfriend der Freund

bra der BH

brake (n) die Bremse

brake (v) bremsen

bread das Brot

break brechen; **to break one's leg** sich das Bein brechen

break down (car) eine Panne haben **31, 115**; (person) zusammenbrechen

breakdown (of car) die Panne; (of person) der Zusammenbruch

breakdown service der Pannendienst

breakfast das Frühstück **38**; **to have breakfast** frühstücken

bridge die Brücke

bring bringen

brochure der Prospekt

broken gebrochen

bronchitis die Bronchitis

brother der Bruder

brown braun

brush (for hair) die Bürste; (for painting) der Pinsel

build bauen

building das Gebäude

bump die Beule

bumper die Stoßstange

buoy die Boje

burn (n) die Verbrennung

burn (v) brennen; **to burn oneself** sich verbrennen

burst platzen

bus der Bus **29**

bus route die Busstrecke

bus station der Busbahnhof

bus stop die Bushaltestelle

busy beschäftigt

but aber

butcher's der Metzger

buy kaufen **84, 86**

by (method) mit; (person, cause) von; (time) bis; (place) an; **by car** mit dem Auto

bye! tschüss!

café das Café
cake der Kuchen
call (n) (on phone) der Anruf
call (v) (phone) anrufen **105**; **to be called** (named) heißen
call back (on phone) zurückrufen
camera die Kamera
camper (vehicle) das Wohnmobil
camping das Campen; **to go camping** campen
camping stove der Campingkocher
campsite der Campingplatz **41**
can (n) die Dose
can (v) können; **I can't** ich kann nicht
cancel absagen
cancelled (flight) annulliert
candle die Kerze
can opener der Dosenöffner
car das Auto
caravan der Wohnwagen
card die Karte
car park der Parkplatz; (multi-storey) das Parkhaus
carry tragen
case: in case of emergency im Notfall
cash das Bargeld; **to pay cash** bar bezahlen
cashpoint der Geldautomat
castle (fortress) die Burg; (mansion) das Schloss
catch fangen; (train, bus) erreichen; **to catch a cold** sich erkälten
cathedral der Dom
CD die CD
cemetery der Friedhof
centimetre(s) Zentimeter
centre das Zentrum **38**
century das Jahrhundert
chair der Stuhl
chairlift der Sessellift
change (n) der Wechsel; (money) das Wechselgeld **86**

change (v) (money) wechseln **94**, **95**
changing room die Umkleide **88**
channel der Kanal
chapel die Kapelle
charge (n) die Gebühr
charge (v) berechnen
cheap billig
check kontrollieren
check in einchecken
check-in der Check-in **25**
checkout die Kasse
cheers! prost!
chemist's die Apotheke
cheque der Scheck
chest die Brust
child das Kind
chilly kühl
chimney der Schornstein
chin das Kinn
church die Kirche
cigar die Zigarre
cigarette die Zigarette
cigarette paper das Zigarettenpapier
cinema das Kino
circus der Zirkus
city die Stadt
clean (adj) sauber
clean (v) sauber machen; (teeth) putzen
cliff die Klippe
climate das Klima
climbing Klettern
cloakroom die Garderobe
clock die Uhr
close schließen
closed geschlossen
clothes die Bekleidung
club (for golf) der Schläger
clutch die Kupplung
coach der Bus
coast die Küste
coathanger der Kleiderbügel
cockroach die Küchenschabe
coffee der Kaffee
coil (contraceptive) die Spirale

coin die Münze
Coke® die Cola
cold *(n)* *(illness)* die Erkältung; **to have a cold** erkältet sein
cold *(adj)* kalt; **it's cold** es ist kalt; **I'm cold** mir ist kalt
collection die Sammlung
colour die Farbe
comb der Kamm
come kommen
come back zurückkommen
come in hereinkommen
come out herauskommen
comfortable *(shoes, chair)* bequem; *(hotel)* komfortabel
company *(firm)* das Unternehmen
compartment *(in train)* das Abteil
complain sich beschweren
comprehensive insurance die Vollkaskoversicherung
computer der Computer
concert das Konzert **67**
concert hall die Konzerthalle
concession die Ermäßigung **23**, **73**
condom das Kondom
confirm bestätigen
connection die Verbindung **26**
constipated: to be constipated Verstopfung haben
consulate das Konsulat
contact *(n)* der Kontakt
contact *(v)* kontaktieren **104**, **115**
contact lens die Kontaktlinse
contagious ansteckend
contraceptive das Verhütungsmittel
cook kochen
cooked gekocht
cooking: to do the cooking kochen
cool kühl; *(calm)* ruhig; *(fantastic)* cool
corkscrew der Korkenzieher
correct richtig
cost *(n)* die Kosten
cost *(v)* kosten
cotton die Baumwolle

cotton bud das Wattestäbchen
cotton wool die Watte
cough *(n)* der Husten; **to have a cough** Husten haben
cough *(v)* husten
count zählen
country das Land
countryside *(scenery)* die Landschaft; *(rural area)* das Land
course: of course natürlich
cover bedecken
credit card die Kreditkarte **37**, **50**, **86**, **95**
cross *(n)* das Kreuz
cross *(v)* *(street, square)* überqueren
cruise die Rundfahrt
cry *(n)* der Schrei; *(call)* der Ruf
cry *(v)* *(weep)* weinen; *(shout)* schreien
cup die Tasse
currency die Währung
customs der Zoll
cut schneiden; **to cut oneself** sich schneiden
cycle path der Radweg

D

damaged kaputt
damp feucht
dance *(n)* der Tanz
dance *(v)* tanzen
dangerous gefährlich
dark dunkel; **dark blue** dunkelblau
date das Datum; **out of date** *(passport, ticket)* abgelaufen
date from stammen aus
date of birth das Geburtsdatum
daughter die Tochter
day der Tag; **the day after tomorrow** übermorgen; **the day before yesterday** vorgestern
dead tot
deaf taub
dear lieb; **Dear Mr Braun** Lieber Herr Braun; **Dear Susanne** Liebe Susanne

debit card die ec-Karte
December Dezember
declare *(at customs)* deklarieren
deep tief
degree(s) Grad
delay die Verspätung
delayed verspätet
deli das Feinkostgeschäft
dentist der Zahnarzt
deodorant das Deo
department die Abteilung
department store das Kaufhaus
departure *(of train, bus, boat)* die
  Abfahrt; *(of plane)* der Abflug
depend on abhängen von; **that
  depends** das kommt darauf an
deposit die Kaution
dessert die Nachspeise **47**
dessertspoon der Dessertlöffel
develop: to get a film developed
  einen Film entwickeln lassen
diabetes der Diabetes
dialling code die Vorwahl
diarrhoea der Durchfall; **to have
  diarrhoea** Durchfall haben
die sterben
diesel der Diesel
diet die Diät; **to be on a diet** Diät
  machen
different (from) anders (als)
difficult schwierig
digital camera die Digitalkamera
dinner das Abendessen; **to have dinner**
  zu Abend essen
direct direkt
direction die Richtung; **to have a
  good sense of direction** einen guten
  Orientierungssinn haben
directory *(telephone directory)* das
  Telefonbuch
directory enquiries die Auskunft
dirty schmutzig
disabled behindert **116**
disaster die Katastrophe

disco die Disko
discount der Rabatt **73**; **to give
  someone a discount** jemandem
  Rabatt gewähren
discount fare der ermäßigte Preis
dish *(food)* das Gericht; **dish of the day**
  das Tagesgericht
dishes das Geschirr; **to do the dishes**
  das Geschirr spülen
dish towel das Geschirrtuch
dishwasher die Geschirrspülmaschine
disinfect desinfizieren
disposable camera die Einmal-Kamera
disturb stören
diving: to go diving tauchen gehen
do tun, machen; **do you have a light?**
  haben Sie Feuer?
doctor der Arzt **108**
door die Tür
downstairs unten
draught beer das Fassbier
dress: to get dressed sich anziehen
dressing *(for salad)* das Dressing
drink *(n)* das Getränk; **to go for a drink**
  etwas trinken gehen **44**; **to have a
  drink** etwas trinken
drink *(v)* trinken
drinking water das Trinkwasser
drive *(n):* **to go for a drive** spazieren
  fahren
drive *(v)* fahren
driving licence der Führerschein
drops *(medicine)* die Tropfen
drown ertrinken
drugs *(medicine)* die Medikamente;
  (addictive substance) die Drogen
drunk betrunken
dry *(adj)* trocken
dry *(v)* trocknen
dry cleaner's die Trockenreinigung
duck *(bird)* die Ente
during während; **during the week**
  unter der Woche
dustbin die Mülltonne

each (one) jeder, jede, jedes
ear das Ohr
early früh
earplugs das Ohropax®
earrings die Ohrringe
earth die Erde
east der Osten; **in the east** im Osten;
   (to the) east of östlich von
Easter Ostern
easy einfach
eat essen **44**
economy class die Touristenklasse
Elastoplast® das Hansaplast®
electric elektrisch
electricity der Strom
electricity meter der Stromzähler
electric shaver der elektrische
   Rasierapparat
e-mail die E-Mail
e-mail address die E-Mail-Adresse **17, 99**
embassy die Botschaft
emergency der Notfall **115; in an
   emergency** im Notfall
emergency exit der Notausgang
empty leer
end das Ende; **at the end of May** Ende
   Mai; **at the end of the street** am Ende
   der Straße
engaged *(toilet, telephone)* besetzt;
   (couple) verlobt
engine der Motor
England England
English *(n) (language)* Englisch; **the
   English** *(people)* die Engländer
English *(adj)* englisch; **I'm English** ich
   bin Engländer/*(female)* Engländerin
enjoy genießen; **enjoy your meal!**
   guten Appetit!; **to enjoy oneself** sich
   amüsieren
enough genug; **that's enough** das reicht
entrance der Eingang
envelope der Umschlag

epileptic der Epileptiker; *(female)* die
   Epileptikerin
equipment die Ausrüstung
espresso der Espresso
euro der Euro
Eurocheque der Euroscheck
Europe Europa
European *(n)* der Europäer; *(female)* die
   Europäerin
European *(adj)* europäisch
evening der Abend; **in the evening**
   abends
every jeder, jede, jedes; **every day**
   täglich
everybody, everyone jeder
everywhere überall; *(go)* überallhin
except außer
exceptional außergewöhnlich
exchange *(currency, goods in shop)*
   umtauschen
exchange rate der Wechselkurs
excuse *(n)* die Entschuldigung
excuse *(v)* entschuldigen; **excuse me**
   Entschuldigung
exhausted erschöpft
exhaust (pipe) der Auspuff
exhibition die Ausstellung **72**
exit der Ausgang
expensive teuer
express letter der Eilbrief
extra zusätzlich
eye das Auge

face das Gesicht
facecloth der Waschlappen
fact die Tatsache; **in fact** tatsächlich
faint ohnmächtig werden
fair die Messe
fall fallen; **to fall asleep** einschlafen; **to
   fall ill** krank werden; **to fall in love** sich
   verlieben
family die Familie

fan (*supporter*) der Fan; (*electric*) der Ventilator
far weit; **far from** weit von
fare (*charge*) der Fahrpreis
fast schnell
fast-food restaurant das Fastfood-Restaurant
fat (*adj*) dick
fat (*n*) das Fett
father der Vater
favour der Gefallen; **to do someone a favour** jemandem einen Gefallen tun
favourite Lieblings-
fax das Fax
February Februar
fed up: to be fed up with someone/something jemanden/etwas satt haben
feel sich fühlen; **I feel good/bad** mir geht es gut/schlecht
feeling das Gefühl
ferry die Fähre
festival das Festival
fetch: to go and fetch someone/something jemanden/etwas abholen
fever das Fieber; **to have a fever** Fieber haben
few wenige; **a few** ein paar
fiancé der Verlobte
fiancée die Verlobte
fight der Kampf; (*argument*) der Streit
fill füllen
fill in (*form*) ausfüllen
fill out (*form*) ausfüllen
fill up: to fill up with petrol voll tanken
filling die Füllung
film der Film **92**
finally endlich
find finden
fine (*adj*) gut; **I'm fine** mir geht es gut
fine (*n*) die Geldstrafe
finger der Finger
finish (*complete*) beenden; (*come to an end*) zu Ende sein
fire das Feuer; **fire!** Feuer!

fire brigade die Feuerwehr
fireworks das Feuerwerk
first erste; **first (of all)** zuerst
first class die erste Klasse
first floor der erste Stock; **on the first floor** im ersten Stock
first name der Vorname
fish der Fisch
fish shop das Fischgeschäft
fitting room die Umkleide
fizzy (*water*) mit Kohlensäure
flash der Blitz
flask (*vacuum flask*) die Thermosflasche
flat (*adj*) flach; (*tyre*) platt
flat (*n*) (*apartment*) die Wohnung
flavour der Geschmack
flaw der Fehler
flight der Flug
flip-flops die Flipflops
floor der Boden; (*storey*) der Stock; **on the floor** auf dem Boden
flu die Grippe
fly (*n*) die Fliege
fly (*v*) fliegen
food das Essen
food poisoning die Lebensmittelvergiftung
foot der Fuß
football Fußball
for für; **for an hour** eine Stunde lang
forbidden verboten
forecast die Vorhersage
forehead die Stirn
foreign ausländisch
foreigner der Ausländer; (*female*) die Ausländerin
forest der Wald
fork die Gabel
former früher
forward vorwärts
four-star petrol das verbleite Benzin
fracture der Bruch
fragile zerbrechlich
France Frankreich

free frei
freezer die Tiefkühltruhe; *(in fridge)* das Eisfach
French *(n)* Französisch
French *(adj)* französisch
Friday Freitag
fridge der Kühlschrank
fried gebraten
friend der Freund; *(female)* die Freundin
from von; **from ... to ...** von ... nach ...
front die Vorderseite; **at the front** vorne; **in front of** vor
fry braten
frying pan die Bratpfanne
full voll; **full of** voller
full board die Vollpension
full fare, full price der volle Preis
funfair die Kirmes
fuse die Sicherung

G

gallery die Gallerie
game das Spiel
garage *(for storage)* die Garage; *(repairing cars)* die Werkstatt **31**; *(selling petrol)* die Tankstelle
garden der Garten
gas das Gas
gas cylinder die Gaskartusche
gastric flu die Darmgrippe
gate *(at airport)* das Gate; *(in wall, fence)* das Tor
gauze die Gaze
gay schwul
gearbox das Getriebe
general allgemein
gents (toilet) die Herrentoilette
German *(n)* der/die Deutsche; *(language)* Deutsch
German *(adj)* deutsch
Germany Deutschland
get *(receive)* bekommen; *(fetch)* holen; *(become)* werden

get off *(from train, bus)* aussteigen
get up aufstehen
gift wrap das Geschenkpapier
girl das Mädchen
girlfriend die Freundin
give geben
give back zurückgeben
glass das Glas; **a glass of water/wine** ein Glas Wasser/Wein
glasses die Brille
gluten-free ohne Gluten
go *(on foot)* gehen; *(by vehicle)* fahren; *(by plane)* fliegen; **to go to Berlin/ Germany** nach Berlin/Deutschland fahren/fliegen; **we're going home tomorrow** wir fahren/fliegen morgen nach Hause
go away *(on foot)* weggehen; *(by vehicle)* wegfahren; *(by plane)* wegfliegen
go in hineingehen
golf Golf
golf course der Golfplatz
good gut; **good morning** guten Morgen; **good afternoon** guten Tag; **good evening** guten Abend
goodbye auf Wiedersehen
goodnight gute Nacht
goods die Waren
go out hinausgehen
GP der Allgemeinarzt
grams Gramm
grass das Gras
great *(excellent)* toll
Great Britain Großbritannien
Greece Griechenland
Greek *(n)* *(male)* der Grieche; *(female)* die Griechin; *(language)* Griechisch
Greek *(adj)* griechisch
green grün
grey grau
grocer's das Lebensmittelgeschäft
ground der Boden; **on the ground** auf dem Boden
ground floor das Erdgeschoss

ground sheet der Zeltboden
grow wachsen
guarantee die Garantie
guest der Gast
guest house die Pension
guide der Fremdenführer
guidebook der Reiseführer
guided tour die Führung
gynaecologist der Frauenarzt

H

hair die Haare
hairdresser *(male)* der Friseur; *(female)* die Friseurin
hairdrier der Fön
half halb; **half a litre** ein halber Liter; **half a kilo** ein halbes Kilo; **half an hour** eine halbe Stunde
half-board die Halbpension
half-pint: a half-pint *(beer)* ein kleines Bier
hand die Hand
handbag die Handtasche
handbrake die Handbremse
handicapped behindert
handkerchief das Taschentuch
hand luggage das Handgepäck **26**
hand-made handgemacht
hangover der Kater
happen passieren
happy glücklich
hard hart; *(difficult)* schwer
hat der Hut
hate hassen
have haben
have to müssen; **I have to go** ich muss gehen
hay fever der Heuschnupfen
he er
head der Kopf
headache die Kopfschmerzen; **to have a headache** Kopfschmerzen haben
headlight der Scheinwerfer

health die Gesundheit
hear hören
heart das Herz
heart attack der Herzanfall
heat die Hitze
heating die Heizung
heavy schwer
hello hallo
helmet der Helm
help *(n)* die Hilfe; **to call for help** um Hilfe rufen; **help!** Hilfe!
help *(v)* helfen **114**
her *(accusative)* sie; *(dative)* ihr; *(possessive)* ihr, ihre
here hier; **here is/are** hier ist/sind
hers: it's hers es gehört ihr; **a friend of hers** ein Freund/*(female)* eine Freundin von ihr
herself sich; *(she herself)* (sie) selbst
hi! hallo!
hi-fi die Hi-Fi-Anlage
high hoch
high blood pressure der Bluthochdruck
high tide die Flut
hiking: to go hiking wandern gehen
hill der Hügel
him *(accusative)* ihn; *(dative)* ihm
himself sich; *(he himself)* (er) selbst
hip die Hüfte
hire mieten **32**, **77**, **79**, **80**
his sein; **it's his** es gehört ihm; **a friend of his** ein Freund/*(female)* eine Freundin von ihm
hitchhike trampen
hold halten
hold on! *(on the phone)* bleiben Sie bitte dran
holiday(s) der Urlaub; **to be on holiday** Urlaub machen
holiday camp das Feriendorf
Holland Holland
home das Zuhause; **at home** zu Hause; **to go home** nach Hause gehen/fahren/ fliegen

homosexual homosexuell
honest ehrlich
honeymoon die Hochzeitsreise
horse das Pferd
hospital das Krankenhaus
hot heiß; **it's hot** es ist heiß; **I'm hot** mir ist heiß; **hot drink** das heiße Getränk
hot chocolate die heiße Schokolade
hotel das Hotel
hotplate die Kochplatte
hour die Stunde; **an hour and a half** eineinhalb Stunden
house das Haus
housework die Hausarbeit; **to do the housework** die Hausarbeit machen
how wie; **how are you?** wie geht es Ihnen?
hunger der Hunger
hungry: to be hungry Hunger haben
hurry: to be in a hurry es eilig haben
hurry (up)! Beeilung!
hurt: it hurts es tut weh; **my head hurts** mein Kopf tut weh
husband der Mann

I

I ich; **I'm English** ich bin Engländer/ (female) Engländerin; **I'm 22 (years old)** ich bin 22 (Jahre alt)
ice das Eis
ice cream das Eis
ice cube der Eiswürfel
identity card der Personalausweis
identity papers die Ausweispapiere
if wenn
ill krank
illness die Krankheit
important wichtig
in in; **in England** in England; **in 2006** 2006; **in German** auf Deutsch; **in the 19th century** im 19. Jahrhundert; **in an hour** in einer Stunde
included inbegriffen

independent unabhängig
indicator (on car) der Blinker
infection die Infektion
information die Information **71**
injection die Spritze
injured verletzt
insect das Insekt
insecticide das Insektengift
inside in; **to be inside** (indoors) drinnen sein
insomnia die Schlaflosigkeit
instant coffee der Pulverkaffee
instead stattdessen; **instead of** anstatt
insurance die Versicherung
intend beabsichtigen
international international
international money order die internationale Zahlungsanweisung
Internet das Internet
Internet café das Internetcafé **99**
invite einladen
Ireland Irland
Irish irisch; **I'm Irish** ich bin Ire/(female) Irin; **the Irish** die Iren
iron (n) das Eisen; (for clothes) das Bügeleisen
iron (v) bügeln
island die Insel
it es; **it's beautiful** es ist schön; **it's warm** es ist warm
Italian (n) (male) der Italiener; (female) die Italienerin; (language) Italienisch
Italian (adj) italienisch
Italy Italien
itchy: it's itchy es juckt
item der Gegenstand

J

jacket die Jacke
January Januar
jetlag der Jetlag
jeweller's der Juwelier
jewellery der Schmuck

job die Stelle
jogging Joggen
journey die Reise
jug der Krug
juice der Saft
July Juli
jumper der Pulli
June Juni
just *(only)* nur; *(recently, at the moment)* gerade; *(exactly)* genau; **just now** gerade eben; **just a little** nur ein bisschen; **just one** nur eins; **I've just arrived** ich bin gerade angekommen; **just in case** für alle Fälle

K

kayak der Kajak
keep *(retain)* behalten; *(remain)* bleiben; **to keep a seat** einen Platz freihalten
key der Schlüssel **31**, **38**, **40**
kidney die Niere
kill töten
kilo(s) Kilo
kilometre(s) Kilometer
kind: what kind of …? was für ein …?
kitchen die Küche
knee das Knie
knife das Messer
knock down *(person with car)* anfahren; *(building)* abreißen
know wissen; **I don't know** ich weiß nicht

L

ladies (toilet) die Damentoilette
lake der See
lamp die Lampe
landmark das Wahrzeichen
landscape die Landschaft
language die Sprache
laptop das Laptop
last *(adj)* letzte; **last year** letztes Jahr
last *(v)* halten; *(be enough)* reichen

late spät
latte der Milchkaffee
laugh lachen
launderette der Waschsalon
lawyer der Anwalt
leaflet der Prospekt
leak undicht sein
learn lernen
least wenigste; **the least** das Mindeste; **at least** zumindest
leave *(go)* gehen; *(by train, bus)* abfahren; *(a room)* verlassen; *(leave behind)* liegen lassen; **to leave open** offen lassen
left linke; **to the left (of)** links (von)
left-luggage (office) die Gepäckaufbewahrung
leg das Bein
lend leihen
lens die Linse
less weniger; **less than** weniger als
let lassen; *(rent out)* vermieten
letter der Brief
letterbox der Briefkasten
library die Bücherei
life das Leben
lift *(elevator)* der Aufzug **38**; **can you give me a lift?** können Sie mich mitnehmen?
light *(adj) (not heavy)* leicht; *(not dark)* hell; **light blue** hellblau
light *(n)* das Licht; **do you have a light?** haben Sie Feuer?
light *(v)* anzünden
light bulb die Glühbirne
lighter das Feuerzeug
lighthouse der Leuchtturm
like *(prep)* wie
like *(v)* mögen **18**; **I'd like …** ich möchte …
line *(mark)* die Linie
lip die Lippe
listen zuhören
listings magazine der Veranstaltungskalender
litre(s) Liter

little *(small)* klein; *(not much)* wenig
live leben
liver die Leber
living room das Wohnzimmer
local time die Ortszeit
lock *(n)* das Schloss
lock *(v)* abschließen
long lang; **a long time** lange; **how long?** wie lange?
look *(seem)* aussehen; **to look tired** müde aussehen
look after sich kümmern um
look at ansehen
look for suchen
lorry der Lastwagen
lose verlieren **115**; **to get lost** *(lose one's way)* sich verlaufen; **to be lost** *(have lost one's way)* sich verlaufen haben
lot: a lot (of) viel
loud laut
love *(n)* die Liebe
love *(v)* lieben
low niedrig
low blood pressure der niedrige Blutdruck
low-fat fettarm
low tide die Ebbe
luck das Glück
lucky: to be lucky Glück haben
luggage das Gepäck **26**
lukewarm lauwarm
lunch das Mittagessen; **to have lunch** zu Mittag essen
lung die Lunge
Luxembourg Luxemburg
luxury *(n)* der Luxus
luxury *(adj)* Luxus-

M

magazine die Zeitschrift
maiden name der Mädchenname
main Haupt-; **main course** das Hauptgericht
make machen

man der Mann
manage schaffen; **to manage to do something** es schaffen, etwas zu tun
manager *(of shop, company)* der Geschäftsführer
many viele; **how many?** wie viele?; **how many times?** wie oft?
map *(of area)* die Karte; *(of town)* der Stadtplan **12**, **28**, **65**, **71**
March März
marina der Jachthafen
market der Markt
married verheiratet
mass *(in church)* die Messe
match *(for striking)* das Streichholz; *(game)* das Spiel
material das Material
matter: it doesn't matter das macht nichts
mattress die Matratze
May Mai
maybe vielleicht
me *(accusative)* mich; *(dative)* mir; **me too** ich auch
meal das Mahlzeit
mean bedeuten; **what does … mean?** was bedeutet …?
medicine das Medikament
medium mittlere; *(meat)* medium
meet treffen **65**
meeting das Treffen
member das Mitglied
menu *(list)* die Speisekarte; *(dishes)* das Menü
message die Nachricht **104**
meter *(in taxi)* der Taxameter; *(for parking)* die Parkuhr
metre(s) Meter
microwave die Mikrowelle
midday der Mittag
middle mittlere; **in the middle** in der Mitte; **in the middle of the night** mitten in der Nacht; **in the middle of the street** mitten auf der Straße

midnight die Mitternacht

might: it might rain es könnte regnen

mill die Mühle

mind: I don't mind es ist mir egal

mine: it's mine es gehört mir; **a friend of mine** ein Freund/(female) eine Freundin von mir

mineral water das Mineralwasser

minister (politician) der Minister

minute die Minute; **at the last minute** in letzter Minute

mirror der Spiegel

Miss Frau

miss (fail to catch or find) verpassen; (absent person or thing) vermissen; **there are two … missing** es fehlen zwei …

mistake der Fehler; **to make a mistake** einen Fehler machen

mobile (phone) das Handy

modern modern

moisturizer die Feuchtigkeitscreme

moment der Moment; **at the moment** im Moment

monastery das Kloster

Monday Montag

money das Geld **84**

month der Monat

monument das Denkmal

mood: to be in a good/bad mood gut/schlecht gelaunt sein

moon der Mond

moped das Moped

more mehr; **more than** mehr als; **much more, a lot more** viel mehr; **there's no more …** es gibt kein(e) … mehr

morning der Morgen

morning-after pill die Pille danach

mosque die Moschee

mosquito die Mücke

most (the majority of) meiste; (to the greatest degree) am meisten; **most people** die meisten

mother die Mutter

motorbike das Motorrad

motorway die Autobahn

mountain der Berg

mountain bike das Mountainbike

mountain hut die Berghütte

mouse die Maus

mouth der Mund

movie der Film

Mr Herr

Mrs Frau

much viel; **how much is it?, how much does it cost?** wie viel kostet das?

muscle der Muskel

museum das Museum

music die Musik

must müssen; **it must be five o'clock** es muss fünf Uhr sein; **I must go** ich muss gehen

my mein

myself (accusative) mich; (dative) mir; (I myself) (ich) selbst

N

nail der Nagel

naked nackt

name der Name; **my name is …** ich heiße …

nap das Nickerchen; **to have a nap** ein Nickerchen machen

napkin die Serviette

nappy die Windel

national holiday der Nationalfeiertag

nature die Natur

near nah; **near the beach** nah am Strand; **the nearest …** der/die/das nächste …

necessary notwendig

neck der Hals

need brauchen

neighbour der Nachbar

neither: neither do I ich auch nicht; **neither … nor …** weder … noch …

nervous nervös

Netherlands: the Netherlands die Niederlande

never nie

new neu

news die Nachrichten

newsagent's der Zeitungsladen

newspaper die Zeitung

newsstand der Zeitungskiosk

next nächste

New Year Neujahr

nice nett

night die Nacht **37**, **39**

nightclub die Disko

nightdress das Nachthemd

no *(as answer)* nein; *(not any)* kein; **no, thank you** nein, danke; **no idea** keine Ahnung

nobody niemand

noise *(sound)* das Geräusch; *(loud sound)* der Krach; **to make a noise** Krach machen

noisy laut

non-drinking water kein Trinkwasser

none keiner, keine, keines; **none of this** nichts davon

non-smoker der Nichtraucher

noon der Mittag

no one niemand

north der Norden; **in the north** im Norden; **(to the) north of** nördlich von

nose die Nase

not nicht; **not yet** noch nicht; **not any** kein; **not at all** überhaupt nicht

note *(something written)* die Notiz; *(of music)* die Note; *(money)* der Schein

notebook das Notizbuch

nothing nichts

novel der Roman

November November

now jetzt

nowadays heutzutage

nowhere nirgends

number die Zahl; *(of telephone, house)* die Nummer

nurse die Krankenschwester; *(male)* der Krankenpfleger

obvious offensichtlich

ocean das Meer

o'clock Uhr; **three o'clock** drei Uhr

October Oktober

of von

offer *(n)* das Angebot

offer *(v)* anbieten

often oft

oil das Öl

ointment die Salbe

OK okay

old alt; **how old are you?** wie alt bist du?; **old people** ältere Leute

old town die Altstadt

on auf; **on foot** zu Fuß; **to be on the train/plane** im Zug/Flugzeug sitzen; **on Thursday** am Donnerstag

once einmal; **once a day/an hour** einmal täglich/in der Stunde

one *(the number 1)* eins; *(before nouns)* ein, eine; **one thousand** tausend

only nur

open *(adj)* offen; *(shop)* geöffnet

open *(v)* öffnen

operate on *(in hospital)* operieren

operation die Operation; **to have an operation** operiert werden

opinion die Meinung; **in my opinion** meiner Meinung nach

opportunity die Gelegenheit

opposite: the opposite das Gegenteil; **opposite the post office** gegenüber der Post

optician der Optiker

or oder

orange *(n)* *(fruit)* die Orange

orange *(adj)* orange

orchestra das Orchester

order *(n)* *(in restaurant, shop)* die Bestellung; **out of order** außer Betrieb

order *(v)* *(in restaurant, shop)* bestellen **46**

organic Bio-

organize organisieren

other andere; **others** andere

otherwise (differently) anders; (in other respects, or else) sonst

our unser

ours: it's ours es gehört uns; **a friend of ours** ein Freund/(female) eine Freundin von uns

out-of-hours pharmacist die Notdienstapotheke

outside draußen; **outside London** außerhalb von London

outward journey (on train, bus) die Hinfahrt; (in plane) der Hinflug

oven der Ofen

over über; (on the other side of) auf der anderen Seite von; **over there** dort drüben

overdone (exaggerated) übertrieben; (steak) verbraten; (vegetables) verkocht

overweight: my luggage is overweight mein Gepäck hat Übergewicht

owe schulden **50**, **85**

own (adj) eigen; **my own car** mein eigenes Auto

own (v) besitzen

owner der Besitzer

P

pack packen

package holiday der Pauschalurlaub

packed lunch das Lunchpaket

packet (of cigarettes) die Schachtel; (of biscuits, tea, washing powder etc) die Packung

painting das Gemälde

pair das Paar; **a pair of shorts** ein Paar Shorts

palace der Palast

paper das Papier; **paper napkin** die Papierserviette; **paper tissue** das Papiertaschentuch

parcel (small) das Päckchen; (big) das Paket

pardon? wie bitte?

parents die Eltern

park (n) der Park

park (v) parken

parking space der Parkplatz

part der Teil

party (celebration) die Party; (political) die Partei

pass (n) der Pass

pass (v) (walk past) vorbeigehen; (drive past) vorbeifahren; (overtake) überholen

passenger der Passagier

passport der Pass

past (time) nach; **a quarter past ten** Viertel nach zehn

path der Weg **79**

patient der Patient; (female) die Patientin

patio die Terrasse

pay bezahlen **85**

pedestrian der Fußgänger

pedestrian precinct die Fußgängerzone

pee pinkeln

peel schälen

pen (ballpoint pen) der Kugelschreiber; (fountain pen) der Füller

pencil der Bleistift

people die Leute; (nation) das Volk

percent Prozent

perfect perfekt

perfume das Parfüm

perhaps vielleicht

period die Periode

person die Person

personal stereo der Walkman®

petrol das Benzin

petrol station die Tankstelle **31**

phone (n) das Telefon

phone (v) anrufen

phone box die Telefonzelle

phone call der Anruf; **to make a phone call** jemanden anrufen

phonecard die Telefonkarte **103**

phone number die Telefonnummer

photo das Foto; **to take a photo (of…)** ein Foto (von …) machen **91**; **to take someone's photo** jemanden fotografieren

picnic das Picknick; **to have a picnic** picknicken

pie *(meat, fish)* die Pastete; *(fruit)* der Kuchen

piece das Stück; **a piece of** ein Stück; **a piece of fruit** ein Stück Obst

piles *(illness)* die Hämorrhoiden

pill die Pille; **to be on the pill** die Pille nehmen

pillow das Kopfkissen

pillowcase der Kopfkissenbezug

PIN (number) die PIN

pink rosa

pity: it's a pity schade

place der Ort

plan der Plan

plane das Flugzeug

plant die Pflanze

plaster (cast) der Gips

plastic das Plastik

plastic bag die Plastiktüte

plate der Teller

platform *(in railway station)* das Gleis **29**

play *(n) (in theatre)* das Stück

play *(v)* spielen

please bitte

pleased erfreut; **pleased to meet you!** sehr erfreut!

pleasure das Vergnügen; **it's a pleasure** gern geschehen

plug *(electrical)* der Stecker; *(in bath, sink)* der Stöpsel

plug in einstecken

plumber der Installateur

point der Punkt; *(sharp end)* die Spitze; *(socket)* die Steckdose

police die Polizei

policeman der Polizist

police station das Polizeirevier

policewoman die Polizistin

poor arm

port *(harbour)* der Hafen; *(wine)* der Portwein

portrait das Porträt

Portugal Portugal

Portuguese *(n) (male)* der Portugiese; *(female)* die Portugiesin; *(language)* Portugiesisch

Portuguese *(adj)* portugiesisch

possible möglich

post *(n) (mail)* die Post

post *(v) (send)* abschicken; *(put in postbox)* einwerfen

postbox der Briefkasten **97**

postcard die Postkarte

postcode die Postleitzahl

poste restante postlagernd

poster das Plakat

postman der Briefträger

post office die Post

pot *(for tea, coffee)* die Kanne; *(for flowers, cooking)* der Topf

pound das Pfund

powder das Puder

practical praktisch

pram der Kinderwagen

prefer lieber mögen

pregnant schwanger **110**

prepare vorbereiten; *(meal)* zubereiten

prescription das Rezept

present *(gift)* das Geschenk

press drücken

pressure der Druck

previous früher

price der Preis

private privat

prize der Preis

probably wahrscheinlich

problem das Problem

procession der Umzug; *(religious)* die Prozession

product das Produkt

profession der Beruf

programme das Programm
promise versprechen
propose vorschlagen
protect schützen
proud (of) stolz (auf)
public öffentlich; **the public** die Öffentlichkeit
public holiday der gesetzliche Feiertag
pull ziehen
purple lila
purpose: on purpose absichtlich
purse das Portmonnaie
push drücken; *(bicycle, pram)* schieben
pushchair der Buggy
put *(upright)* stellen; *(flat)* legen; **put it in your bag** steck es in deine Tasche
put out *(light, fire)* ausmachen; *(shoulder, knee)* sich ausrenken
put up *(hand)* heben; *(umbrella)* aufklappen; *(picture)* aufhängen; *(tent)* aufschlagen
pyjamas der Pyjama

Q

quality die Qualität; **of good/bad quality** von guter/schlechter Qualität
quarter das Viertel; **a quarter of an hour** eine Viertelstunde; **a quarter to ten** Viertel vor zehn
quay der Kai
question die Frage
queue *(n)* die Schlange
queue *(v)* Schlange stehen
quick schnell
quickly schnell
quiet ruhig
quite ziemlich; **quite a lot of** ziemlich viel(e)

R

racist der Rassist; *(female)* die Rassistin
racket *(for sports)* der Schläger

radiator die Heizung
radio das Radio
radio station der Radiosender
rain *(n)* der Regen
rain *(v)* regnen; **it's raining** es regnet
raincoat der Regenmantel
rape *(n)* die Vergewaltigung
rape *(v)* vergewaltigen
rare selten; *(meat)* blutig
rarely selten
rather ziemlich
raw roh
razor der Rasierapparat
razor blade die Rasierklinge
reach erreichen
read lesen
ready fertig
reasonable vernünftig
receipt die Quittung **86**, **111**
receive *(letter, present)* erhalten; *(guest, on radio/television)* empfangen
reception *(in hotel)* die Rezeption; *(on mobile phone)* der Empfang; **at reception** an der Rezeption
receptionist der Herr/*(female)* die Dame an der Rezeption
recipe das Rezept
recognize erkennen
recommend empfehlen
red rot
red light die rote Ampel
reduce reduzieren
reduction die Reduzierung
red wine der Rotwein
refrigerator der Kühlschrank
refund *(n)* die Erstattung; **to get a refund** sein Geld zurückbekommen **89**
refund *(v)* erstatten
refuse ablehnen
registered: by registered post per Einschreiben
registration number das Kennzeichen
remember *(recollect)* sich erinnern an; *(not forget)* denken an

remind erinnern

remove (clothes, hat) ablegen

rent (n) die Miete

rent (v) (tenant) mieten; (owner) vermieten **40**

rental car der Mietwagen

repair reparieren **32**; **to get something repaired** etwas reparieren lassen

repeat wiederholen **9**

reserve reservieren **45**

reserved reserviert

rest (n) (what remains) der Rest; (break) die Pause

rest (v) (relax) sich ausruhen

restaurant das Restaurant

return (n) (ticket) die Rückfahrkarte; (arrival back) die Rückkehr

return (v) (come back) zurückkehren

reverse-charge call das R-Gespräch **103**

reverse gear der Rückwärtsgang

rheumatism das Rheuma

rib die Rippe

right (n) (entitlement) das Recht; (right-hand side) die rechte Seite; **to the right (of)** rechts (von)

right (adj) (correct, correctly) richtig; (not left) rechte; **right away** sofort; **right here** genau hier

ring (n) (jewellery, circle) der Ring; **to give someone a ring** (phone) jemanden anrufen

ring (v) (phone) anrufen; (bell) klingeln

ripe reif

rip-off der Nepp

risk das Risiko

river der Fluss

road die Straße

road sign das Schild

rock (boulder) der Felsen; (substance) der Stein

rollerblades die Inliner

room das Zimmer **37**, **38**

rosé (wine) der Rosé

round (in shape) rund; (surrounding) um ... herum; **round here** hier in der Nähe

roundabout (on road) der Kreisverkehr; (at fairground) das Karussell

rubbish (waste) der Müll; (nonsense) der Unsinn; **to take the rubbish out** den Müll hinausbringen

rucksack der Rucksack

rug (carpet) der Teppich; (blanket) die Decke

ruins die Ruinen; **in ruins** zerstört

run out: we've run out of petrol wir haben kein Benzin mehr

S

sad traurig

safe sicher; **have a safe journey!** gute Reise!

safety die Sicherheit

safety belt der Sicherheitsgurt

sail (n) das Segel

sail (v) segeln

sailing: to go sailing segeln gehen

sale der Verkauf; **for sale** zu verkaufen

sales der Ausverkauf

salt das Salz

salted gesalzen

salty salzig

same gleiche; **the same** das Gleiche

sand der Sand

sandals die Sandalen

sanitary towel die Damenbinde

Saturday Samstag

saucepan der Kochtopf

save (money, time) sparen; (rescue) retten; (on computer) speichern

say sagen; **how do you say ...?** was heißt ...?

scared: to be scared (of) Angst haben (vor)

scenery die Landschaft

scissors die Schere

scoop (of ice cream) die Kugel

scooter der Roller
Scot der Schotte; *(female)* die Schottin
scotch *(whisky)* der Scotch
Scotland Schottland
Scottish schottisch
scuba diving Sporttauchen
sea das Meer
seafood die Meeresfrüchte
seasick seekrank
seaside: at the seaside am Meer
seaside resort der Badeort
season *(time of year)* die Jahreszeit; *(for holidays)* die Saison
seat der Platz **24**
sea view der Meeresblick
seaweed die Algen
second *(n) (in time)* die Sekunde
second *(adj)* zweite
secondary school die höhere Schule
second class die zweite Klasse
second-hand gebraucht
secure sicher
security die Sicherheit
see sehen; **see you later!** bis später!; **see you soon!** bis bald!; **see you tomorrow!** bis morgen!
seem scheinen; **it seems that ...** es scheint ...
seldom selten
self-confidence das Selbstbewusstsein
sell verkaufen
Sellotape® das Klebeband
send schicken
sender der Absender
sense der Sinn; **to make sense** Sinn haben
sensitive empfindlich
sentence *(words)* der Satz
separate trennen
separately getrennt
September September
serious ernst
several mehrere
sex *(intercourse)* der Sex; *(gender)* das Geschlecht

shade der Schatten; **in the shade** im Schatten
shame: it's a shame, what a shame schade
shampoo das Shampoo
shape die Form
share teilen
shave sich rasieren
shaving cream die Rasiercreme
shaving foam der Rasierschaum
she sie
sheet *(for bed)* das Laken; *(of paper)* das Blatt
shellfish die Meeresfrüchte
shirt das Hemd
shock der Schock; *(electric)* der Schlag
shocking furchtbar
shoes die Schuhe
shop das Geschäft
shop assistant der Verkäufer; *(female)* die Verkäuferin
shopkeeper der Ladenbesitzer; *(female)* die Ladenbesitzerin
shopping *(items bought)* die Einkäufe; **to do some/the shopping** einkaufen gehen
shopping centre das Einkaufszentrum
short kurz; **I'm two euros short** mir fehlen zwei Euro
short cut die Abkürzung
shorts die Shorts
short-sleeved kurzärmelig
shoulder die Schulter
show *(n)* die Show
show *(v)* zeigen
shower *(wash)* die Dusche; *(rain)* der Schauer; **to take a shower** duschen
shower gel das Duschgel
shut *(close)* schließen; *(closed)* geschlossen
shuttle der Shuttle
shy schüchtern
sick schlecht; **I feel sick** mir ist schlecht
side die Seite

sign (n) (symbol, gesture) das Zeichen; (road/shop sign) das Schild

sign (v) unterschreiben

signal das Signal

signature die Unterschrift

silent still

silver das Silber

silver-plated versilbert

since seit

sing singen

singer der Sänger; (female) die Sängerin

single (only one) einzig; (not double) Einzel-; (unmarried) unverheiratet

single (ticket) die einfache Fahrkarte

sister die Schwester

sit down sich hinsetzen

size die Größe

skis die Skier

ski boots die Skistiefel

skiing: to go skiing skifahren gehen

ski lift der Skilift

ski pole der Skistock

ski resort der Skiort

skin die Haut

skirt der Rock

sky der Himmel

skyscraper der Wolkenkratzer

sleep (n) der Schlaf

sleep (v) schlafen; **to sleep with** schlafen mit

sleeping bag der Schlafsack

sleeping pill die Schlaftablette

sleepy: to be sleepy müde sein

sleeve der Ärmel

slice die Scheibe

sliced in Scheiben

slide (photo) das Dia; (in playground) die Rutsche

slow langsam

slowly langsam

small klein

smell (n) der Geruch

smell (v) riechen; **to smell good/bad** gut/schlecht riechen

smile (n) das Lächeln

smile (v) lächeln

smoke (n) der Rauch

smoke (v) rauchen

smoker der Raucher; (female) die Raucherin

snack der Imbiss

snow (n) der Schnee

snow (v) schneien; **it's snowing** es schneit

so so; **so that** sodass

soap die Seife

socks die Socken

some manche; **some people** manche Leute

somebody, someone jemand

something etwas; **something else** etwas anderes

sometimes manchmal

somewhere irgendwo; **somewhere else** irgendwo anders

son der Sohn

song das Lied

soon bald

sore: to have a sore throat Halsschmerzen haben

sorry! Entschuldigung!

south der Süden; **in the south** im Süden; **(to the) south of** südlich von

souvenir das Andenken

Spain Spanien **Spaniard** der Spanier (female) die Spanierin

Spanish (n) Spanisch

Spanish (adj) spanisch

spare zusätzlich

spare part das Ersatzteil

spare tyre der Reservereifen

spare wheel das Reserverad

spark plug die Zündkerze

speak sprechen **10, 104**

special speziell

speciality die Spezialität

speed die Geschwindigkeit; **at full speed** mit Höchstgeschwindigkeit

spell *(word)* schreiben; *(aloud)* buchstabieren **10**

spend *(money)* ausgeben; *(time)* verbringen

spice das Gewürz

spicy würzig

spider die Spinne

splinter der Splitter

split up sich trennen

spoil *(ruin)* verderben; *(person)* verwöhnen

sponge *(for cleaning, washing)* der Schwamm; *(cake)* der Biskuit

spoon der Löffel

sport der Sport

sports ground der Sportplatz

sporty sportlich

spot *(mark)* der Fleck; *(pimple)* der Pickel; *(place)* der Ort

sprain: to sprain one's ankle sich den Knöchel verstauchen

spring *(season)* der Frühling

square *(in town)* der Platz

stadium das Stadion

stain der Fleck

stairs die Treppe

stamp *(for letter)* die Briefmarke **97**

start anfangen

state *(country)* der Staat; *(condition)* der Zustand

statement die Aussage

station *(for trains)* der Bahnhof; *(for buses)* der Busbahnhof; *(radio, television station)* der Sender

stay *(n)* der Aufenthalt

stay *(v)* *(remain)* bleiben; *(in hotel etc)* übernachten; **to stay in touch** in Kontakt bleiben

steal stehlen **115**

step *(pace)* der Schritt; *(of stairs)* die Stufe

sticking plaster das Heftpflaster

still *(with time)* noch; *(nevertheless)* trotzdem; *(motionless)* still

still water das stille Wasser

sting *(n)* *(wound)* der Stich

sting *(v)* stechen; **to get stung (by)** gestochen werden (von)

stock: out of stock nicht vorrätig

stomach der Magen

stone der Stein

stop *(n)* *(where bus, tram, train stops)* die Haltestelle **29**; *(stay)* der Aufenthalt; *(break)* der Halt; **to make a stop** Halt machen

stop *(v)* *(vehicle)* anhalten; *(stay)* bleiben; *(take a break)* Halt machen

storey der Stock

storm der Sturm

straight ahead, straight on geradeaus

strange seltsam

street die Straße

strong stark

stuck eingeklemmt; **I'm stuck** ich sitze fest; **the door's stuck** die Tür klemmt

student der Student; *(female)* die Studentin **23**

studies das Studium

study studieren

style der Stil

subtitled mit Untertiteln

suburb der Vorort

suffer leiden

suggest *(propose)* vorschlagen

suit: does that suit you? passt Ihnen das?

suitcase der Koffer **26**

summer der Sommer

summit der Gipfel

sun die Sonne; **in the sun** in der Sonne

sunbathe sich sonnen

sunburnt: to get sunburnt einen Sonnenbrand bekommen

sun cream die Sonnencreme

Sunday Sonntag

sunglasses die Sonnenbrille

sunhat der Sonnenhut

sunrise der Sonnenaufgang

sunset der Sonnenuntergang

sunstroke der Sonnenstich; **to get sunstroke** einen Sonnenstich bekommen
supermarket der Supermarkt **41**
supplement (in train) der Zuschlag
sure sicher
surf surfen
surfboard das Surfbrett
surfing: to go surfing surfen gehen
surgical spirit der Alkohol
surname der Nachname
surprise (n) die Überraschung
surprise (v) überraschen
sweat schwitzen
sweater der Pulli
sweet (n) (candy) die Süßigkeit; (dessert) die Nachspeise
sweet (adj) süß
swim schwimmen; **to go for a swim** schwimmen gehen
swimming pool das Schwimmbad; (in hotel) der Swimmingpool
swimming trunks die Badehose
swimsuit der Badeanzug
switchboard operator der Telefonist; (female) die Telefonistin
switch off ausschalten
switch on anschalten
swollen geschwollen
synagogue die Synagoge
syrup der Sirup

T

table der Tisch
tablet die Tablette
take nehmen; **it takes two hours** es dauert zwei Stunden
takeaway (restaurant) der Imbiss; (meal) das Essen zum Mitnehmen
take off (plane) starten
talk sprechen
tall (person) groß; (building) hoch
tampon der Tampon

tan braun werden; **to get a tan** braun werden
tanned braun
tap der Wasserhahn
taste (n) der Geschmack
taste (v) (have flavour, experience flavour of) schmecken; (test) probieren
tax die Steuer
tax-free steuerfrei
taxi das Taxi **32**
taxi driver der Taxifahrer; (female) die Taxifahrerin
T-bar der Schlepplift
team das Team
teaspoon der Teelöffel
teenager der Teenager
telephone (n) das Telefon
telephone (v) anrufen
television das Fernsehen
tell sagen; (story) erzählen
temperature die Temperatur; **to have a temperature** Fieber haben; **to take someone's temperature** bei jemandem Fieber messen
temporary vorübergehend
tennis Tennis
tennis court der Tennisplatz
tennis shoes die Tennisschuhe
tent das Zelt
tent peg der Hering
terminal (at airport) das Terminal
terrible furchtbar
thank danken; **thank you** danke; **thank you very much** vielen Dank
thanks danke; **thanks to** dank
that der/die/das; **that one** der/die/das da
the der, die, das
theatre das Theater
theft der Diebstahl
their ihr
theirs: it's theirs es gehört ihnen; **a friend of theirs** ein Freund/(female) eine Freundin von ihnen

them *(accusative)* sie; *(dative)* ihnen
theme park der Vergnügungspark
then *(afterwards)* dann; *(in the past)* damals
there dort; **there is/are ...** es gibt ...
therefore deshalb
thermometer das Thermometer
Thermos® flask die Thermosflasche
these diese
they sie; **they say that ...** man sagt ...
thief der Dieb
thigh der Oberschenkel
thin dünn
thing das Ding; **things** Dinge
think denken
think about nachdenken über
thirst der Durst
thirsty: be thirsty Durst haben
this das; **this one** dieses; **this evening** heute Abend; **this is ...** das ist ...
those diese
throat der Hals
throw werfen
throw out hinauswerfen
Thursday Donnerstag
ticket *(for train, bus)* die Fahrkarte 23; *(for plane)* das Flugticket; *(for museum, concert)* die Eintrittskarte 66, 67
ticket office *(at railway station)* der Fahrkartenschalter; *(at theatre, museum)* die Kasse
tidy ordentlich
tie die Krawatte
tight *(dress, bend)* eng; *(knot)* fest
tights die Strumpfhose
time die Zeit 123; **what time is it?** wie viel Uhr ist es?; **from time to time** von Zeit zu Zeit; **on time** pünktlich; **three/four times** dreimal/viermal
time difference der Zeitunterschied
timetable der Fahrplan 23
tinfoil die Alufolie
tip *(for waiter)* das Trinkgeld; *(end)* die Spitze; *(advice)* der Tipp

tired müde
tobacco der Tabak
tobacconist's das Tabakgeschäft
today heute
together zusammen
toilet die Toilette 45
toilet bag der Kulturbeutel
toilet paper das Toilettenpapier
toiletries die Toilettenartikel
toll *(fee)* die Gebühr
tomorrow morgen; **tomorrow evening** morgen Abend; **tomorrow morning** morgen früh
tongue die Zunge
tonight *(evening)* heute Abend; *(night)* heute Nacht
too *(also)* auch; *(excessively)* zu; **too small** zu klein; **too many** zu viele; **too much** zu viel
tooth der Zahn
toothbrush die Zahnbürste
toothpaste die Zahnpasta
top *(of hill)* der Gipfel; *(of bottle)* der Deckel; *(clothing)* das Oberteil; **at the top** oben
torch *(electric)* die Taschenlampe
touch berühren
tourist der Tourist
tourist office die Touristeninformation
tourist trap die Touristenfalle
towards *(in the direction of)* zu; *(facing)* nach; *(with regard to)* gegenüber
towel das Handtuch
town die Stadt
town centre das Stadtzentrum
town hall die Stadthalle
toy das Spielzeug
traditional traditionell
traffic der Verkehr
traffic jam der Stau
train der Zug 28, 29; **the train to Munich** der Zug nach München
train station der Bahnhof
tram die Straßenbahn

transfer *(of money)* die Überweisung
translate übersetzen
travel agent's das Reisebüro
travel reisen
traveller's cheque der Reisescheck
trip die Reise; **have a good trip!** gute Reise!
trolley *(for luggage)* der Gepäckwagen; *(for shopping)* der Einkaufswagen
trouble: to be in trouble in Schwierigkeiten stecken
trousers die Hose
true wahr
try versuchen; **to try to do something** versuchen, etwas zu tun
try on anprobieren **88**
Tuesday Dienstag
tube *(underground)* die U-Bahn; *(pipe)* das Rohr
tube station die U-Bahn-Station
turn *(v) (in car)* abbiegen
turn *(n)* **: it's your turn** Sie sind dran
twice zweimal
type *(n)* die Art; **what type of ...?** was für ein(e) ...?
type *(v)* tippen
typical typisch
tyre der Reifen

umbrella der Regenschirm
uncomfortable unbequem; **to feel uncomfortable** sich nicht wohl fühlen
under unter
underground die U-Bahn
underground line die U-Bahn-Linie
underground station die U-Bahn-Station
underneath unter
underpants die Unterhose
understand verstehen **10**
underwear die Unterwäsche
United Kingdom Großbritannien und Nordirland

United States: the United States die Vereinigten Staaten
until bis
upset aufgeregt
upstairs oben
urgent dringend
us uns
use benutzen; **I'm used to it** ich bin das gewöhnt
useful nützlich
useless nutzlos; *(pointless)* zwecklos
usually normalerweise
U-turn: to do a U-turn *(in car)* wenden

vaccinated (against) geimpft (gegen)
valid *(document)* gültig
valley das Tal
VAT die Mehrwertsteuer
vegetarian *(n)* der Vegetarier; *(female)* die Vegetarierin
vegetarian *(adj)* vegetarisch
very sehr
view *(from a place)* die Aussicht
villa die Villa
village das Dorf
visa das Visum
visit *(n)* der Besuch
visit *(v)* besuchen
volleyball Volleyball
vomit sich erbrechen

waist die Taille
wait warten; **to wait for someone/ something** auf jemanden/etwas warten
waiter der Kellner
waitress die Kellnerin
wake up aufwachen
Wales Wales
walk gehen; **to go for a walk** spazieren gehen

walking: to go walking wandern gehen
walking boots die Wanderschuhe
Walkman® der Walkman®
wallet die Brieftasche
want wollen; **to want to do something** etwas tun wollen
warm warm
warn warnen
wash waschen; **to wash one's hair** sich die Haare waschen; **to have a wash** sich waschen
washbasin das Waschbecken
washing: to do the washing Wäsche waschen
washing machine die Waschmaschine
washing powder das Waschpulver
washing-up liquid das Spülmittel
wasp die Wespe
waste *(rubbish)* der Abfall
watch *(n)* die Uhr
watch *(v)* *(game, film, play)* sich ansehen; **watch out!** pass auf!
water das Wasser **47**
water heater der Boiler
waterproof wasserdicht
waterskiing Wasserski
wave *(on sea)* die Welle
way *(route)* der Weg; *(direction)* die Richtung
way in der Eingang
way out der Ausgang
we wir
weak schwach
wear *(clothes, hat)* tragen
weather das Wetter **20**, **21**
weather forecast die Wettervorhersage **20**
website die Website
wedding anniversary der Hochzeitstag
Wednesday Mittwoch
week die Woche
weekend das Wochenende
welcome willkommen; **you're welcome** bitte

well gut; **I'm very well** mir geht es sehr gut; **well done** *(meat)* durchgebraten
well-known bekannt
Welsh walisisch; **I'm Welsh** ich bin Waliser/*(female)* Waliserin
west der Westen; **in the west** im Westen; **(to the) west of** westlich von
wet nass
wetsuit der Taucheranzug
what was; **what do you want?** was wollen Sie?
wheel das Rad
wheelchair der Rollstuhl
when *(in questions)* wann; *(specifying time)* wenn; *(in the past)* als
where wo; **where is/are …?** wo ist/sind …?; **where are you from?** woher kommen Sie?; **where are you going?** wohin gehen/fahren Sie?
which welcher, welche, welches
while während; **a while** eine Weile
white weiß
white wine der Weißwein
who wer; **who's calling?** wer ist da?
whole ganze
whose wessen; **whose is it?** wem gehört das?
why warum
wide breit
wife die Frau
wild wild
wind der Wind
window das Fenster; *(of shop)* das Schaufenster; **in the window** im Schaufenster
windscreen die Windschutzscheibe
windsurfing Windsurfen
wine der Wein **47**
winter der Winter
with mit
withdraw *(money)* abheben
without ohne
woman die Frau
wonderful herrlich

wood das Holz; *(forest)* der Wald
wool die Wolle
work *(n)* die Arbeit; *(in art, literature)* das Werk; **work of art** das Kunstwerk
work *(v)* arbeiten
worse schlechter; **to get worse** schlechter werden; **it's worse (than)** es ist schlechter (als)
worth wert; **it's worth it** es lohnt sich; **it's not worth 50 euros** es ist keine 50 Euro wert
wound die Wunde
wrist das Handgelenk
write schreiben **85**
wrong falsch

XYZ

X-rays das Röntgen

year das Jahr
yellow gelb
yes ja
yesterday gestern; **yesterday evening** gestern Abend
you *(familiar single/familiar plural/formal)* du/ihr/Sie; *(accusative)* dich/euch/Sie; *(dative)* dir/euch/Ihnen
young jung
your *(familiar single)* dein; *(familiar plural)* euer; *(formal)* Ihr
yours: it's yours *(familiar single/familiar plural/formal)* es gehört dir/euch/Ihnen; **a friend of yours** *(female)* eine Freundin von dir/euch/Ihnen
youth hostel die Jugendherberge

zero null
zip der Reißverschluss
zoo der Zoo
zoom (lens) das Zoomobjektiv

DICTIONARY

GERMAN-ENGLISH

A

abbiegen turn
Abend evening; **zu Abend essen** to have dinner
Abendessen dinner
abends in the evening
aber but
abfahren leave
Abfahrt departure
Abfall rubbish; waste
Abfalleimer bin
Abflug departure
abgelaufen out of date
abhängen von to depend on
abheben to withdraw
abholen to go and fetch
Abkürzung short cut
ablegen to remove
ablehnen to refuse
abreißen to pull down
absagen to cancel
abschicken to post, to send off
abschließen to lock
Absender sender
absichtlich on purpose
Abtei abbey
Abteil compartment
Abteilung department
Adapter adaptor
Adresse address
Algen seaweed
Alkohol alcohol; surgical spirit
alle all
Allee avenue
allergisch allergic

alles everything
allgemein general
Allgemeinarzt GP
als than; when
alt old; **wie alt bist du?** how old are you?
Alter age
ältere Leute old people
Altstadt old town
Alufolie tinfoil
Ameise ant
Amerika America
Amerikaner, Amerikanerin American
amerikanisch American
amüsieren: sich amüsieren to enjoy oneself
an at; by; on
anbieten to offer
Andenken souvenir
andere other; others; **ein anderer/eine andere/ein anderes** another
anders (als) different (from)
anfahren to knock down
Anfang beginning; **am Anfang** at the beginning
anfangen to begin, to start
Anfänger beginner
Angebot offer
Angst haben (vor) to be scared (of)
anhalten to stop
ankommen to arrive; **das kommt darauf an** that depends
Ankunft arrival
annehmen to accept
annulliert cancelled
anprobieren to try on

Anruf phone call
Anrufbeantworter answering machine
anrufen to call, to phone
anschalten to switch on
Anschrift address
ansehen to look at; **sich einen Film/ein Fußballspiel ansehen** to watch a film/a football match
anstatt instead of
ansteckend contagious
Antibiotika antibiotics
Antwort answer
antworten to answer
Anwalt lawyer
anziehen: sich anziehen to get dressed
anzünden to light
Apotheke chemist's
Après-Lotion after-sun (cream)
Arbeit work
arbeiten to work
Arm arm
arm poor
Ärmel sleeve
Art type
Arzt doctor
Aschenbecher ashtray
auch also, too; **ich auch** me too; **ich auch nicht** neither do I
auf on; **auf Deutsch** in German
Aufenthalt stay
aufgeregt upset; excited
aufhängen to put up; to hang up
aufklappen to open; to put up
aufpassen: pass auf! watch out!
aufschlagen to open; to put up
aufstehen to get up
aufwachen to wake up
Aufzug lift
Auge eye
ausfüllen to fill in
Ausgang exit
ausgeben to spend
Auskunft information; directory enquiries
Ausland: im Ausland abroad; **ins**

Ausland abroad; **aus dem Ausland** from abroad
Ausländer, Ausländerin foreigner
ausländisch foreign
ausleihen to borrow
ausmachen to put out; to turn off
Auspuff exhaust (pipe)
ausrenken: sich die Schulter ausrenken to put one's shoulder out
ausruhen: sich ausruhen to rest
Ausrüstung equipment
Aussage statement
ausschalten to switch off
aussehen to look; **müde aussehen** to look tired
außer except; **außer Betrieb** out of order
außergewöhnlich exceptional
außerhalb: außerhalb von Berlin outside Berlin
Aussicht view
aussteigen to get off
Ausstellung exhibition
Ausverkauf sales
Ausweispapiere identity papers
Auto car
Autobahn motorway

ß

Babyflasche baby's bottle
backen to bake
Bäcker baker's
Bad bathroom; bath; swim
Badeanzug swimsuit
Badehose swimming trunks
baden to have a bath; to swim
Badeort seaside resort
Badetuch bath towel
Badewanne bath
Bahnhof (train) station
bald soon
Balkon balcony
Bank bank; bench
Bar bar

bar: bar bezahlen to pay cash
Bargeld cash
Bart beard
Batterie battery
bauen to build
Baumwolle cotton
beabsichtigen to intend
bedecken to cover
bedeuten to mean; **was bedeutet ...?** what does ... mean?
Beeilung! hurry (up)!
beenden to finish
behalten to keep
behindert disabled, handicapped
bei near; at; **bei meinem Vater** at my father's
beide both; **wir beide** both of us
Bein leg
beißen to bite
bekannt well-known
Bekleidung clothes
bekommen to get
Belgien Belgium
Belgier, Belgierin Belgian
belgisch Belgian
benutzen to use
Benzin petrol
bequem comfortable
berechnen to charge
Berg mountain
Berghütte mountain hut
Beruf profession
berühren to touch
beschäftigt busy
beschweren: sich beschweren to complain
besetzt engaged; taken
besitzen to own
Besitzer owner
besser better; **besser werden** to get better; **es ist besser, wenn ...** it's better to ...
bestätigen to confirm
beste best; **das Beste** the best

bestellen to order
Bestellung order
Besuch visit
besuchen to visit
betrunken drunk
Bett bed
Beule bump
bezahlen to pay
BH bra
Biene bee
billig cheap
Bio- organic
bis until; by; **bis später!** see you later!; **bis bald!** see you soon!; **bis morgen!** see you tomorrow!
Biskuit sponge
Biss bite
bisschen: ein bisschen a bit (of)
bitte please; you're welcome
Blase blister; bladder; bubble
Blatt leaf; sheet
blau blue
bleiben to stay; **bleiben Sie bitte dran** hold on
Bleistift pencil
Blinddarmentzündung appendicitis
Blinker indicator
Blitz flash
Blut blood
Blutdruck blood pressure
bluten to bleed
Bluthochdruck high blood pressure
blutig rare
Boden floor; ground; bottom; **auf dem Boden** on the floor/ground
Boiler water heater
Boje buoy
botanischer Garten botanical garden
Botschaft embassy
braten to fry; to roast
Bratpfanne frying pan
brauchen to need
braun brown; tanned; **braun werden** to get a tan

brechen to break; **sich das Bein brechen** to break one's leg
breit wide
Bremse brake
bremsen to brake
brennen to burn
Brett board
Brief letter
Briefkasten postbox; letterbox
Briefmarke stamp
Brieftasche wallet
Briefträger postman
Brille glasses
bringen to bring
Brot bread
Bruch fracture
Brücke bridge
Bruder brother
Brust chest
Buch book
Bücherei library
Buchhandlung bookshop
buchstabieren to spell
Bügeleisen iron
bügeln to iron
Buggy pushchair
Burg castle
Bürste brush
Bus bus; coach
Busbahnhof bus station
Bushaltestelle bus stop
Busstrecke bus route

C

Campen camping
campen to go camping
Campingkocher camping stove
Campingplatz campsite

D

damals then
Damenbinde sanitary towel

Damen(toilette) ladies (toilet)
Dank: vielen Dank thank you very much
dank thanks to
danke thank you
danken to thank
dann then
Darmgrippe gastric flu
das the; this; that; **das ist ...** this is ...; **das da** that one *(see grammar)*
Datum date
dauern: es dauert zwei Stunden it takes two hours
Decke blanket; ceiling
Deckel lid; top
dein your *(see grammar)*
deklarieren declare
dem (to) the *(see grammar)*
den (to) the *(see grammar)*
denken think; **denken an** think about; remember
Denkmal monument
Deo deodorant
der the; that; **der da** that one *(see grammar)*
deshalb therefore
desinfizieren to disinfect
Dessertlöffel dessertspoon
Deutsch German
deutsch German
Deutsche German
Deutschland Germany
Dezember December
Dia slide
Diät diet; **Diät machen** be on a diet
dich you; yourself *(see grammar)*
dick fat; thick
die the; that; **die da** that one *(see grammar)*
Dieb thief
Diebstahl theft
Dienstag Tuesday
diese this; these; those; **dieses** this one *(see grammar)*

Digitalkamera digital camera
Ding thing; **Dinge** things
dir (to) you; **ein Freund von dir** a friend of yours *(see grammar)*
direkt direct
Disko disco, nightclub
Dom cathedral
Donnerstag Thursday
Dorf village
dort there; **dort drüben** over there
Dose can
Dosenöffner can opener
dran: Sie sind dran it's your turn
draußen outside
dringend urgent
drinnen inside
Drogen drugs
Druck pressure
drücken to press
du you *(see grammar)*
dunkel dark; **dunkelblau** dark blue
dünn thin
Durchfall diarrhoea; **Durchfall haben** to have diarrhoea
durchgebraten well done
Durst thirst; **Durst haben** to be thirsty
Dusche shower
duschen to take a shower
Duschgel shower gel

E

Ebbe low tide
ec-Karte debit card
egal: es ist mir egal I don't mind
ehrlich honest
eigen own; **mein eigenes Auto** my own car
Eilbrief express letter
eilig: es eilig haben to be in a hurry
ein, eine a; one *(see grammar)*
einchecken to check in
einfach easy; **einfache Fahrkarte** single (ticket)

Eingang entrance
eingeklemmt stuck
Einkäufe shopping
einkaufen gehen to do some/the shopping
Einkaufswagen trolley
Einkaufszentrum shopping centre
einladen to invite
einmal once; **einmal täglich/in der Stunde** once a day/an hour
Einmal-Kamera disposable camera
eins one
einschlafen to fall asleep
Einschreiben: per Einschreiben by registered post
einstecken to plug in; to post
Eintritt admission
Eintrittskarte ticket
einwerfen to post; to insert
Einzel- single
einzige only; single
Eis ice; ice cream
Eisen iron
Eisfach freezer (compartment)
Eiswürfel ice cube
elektrisch electric; **elektrischer Rasierapparat** electric shaver
Eltern parents
E-Mail-Adresse e-mail address
Empfang reception
empfangen to receive
empfehlen to recommend
empfindlich sensitive
Ende end; **Ende Mai** at the end of May; **am Ende der Straße** at the end of the street; **zu Ende sein** to finish
endlich finally
eng tight; narrow
England England
Engländer Englishman; **er ist Engländer** he is English; **die Engländer** the English
Engländerin Englishwoman
Englisch English

englisch English
Ente duck
entfernt: zehn Kilometer entfernt
  ten kilometres away
entschuldigen to excuse
Entschuldigung excuse; apology;
  Entschuldigung! excuse me!; sorry!
entwickeln: einen Film entwickeln
  lassen to get a film developed
Epileptiker, Epileptikerin epileptic
er he
erbrechen: sich erbrechen to vomit
Erde earth
Erdgeschoss ground floor
erfreut pleased; **sehr erfreut!** pleased
  to meet you!
erhalten to receive
erinnern to remind; **sich erinnern an**
  to remember
erkälten: sich erkälten to catch a cold;
  erkältet sein to have a cold
Erkältung cold
erkennen to recognize
ermäßigt reduced
Ermäßigung concession
ernst serious
erreichen to reach; to catch
Ersatzteil spare part
erschöpft exhausted
erstatten to refund
Erstattung refund
erste first; **erste Klasse** first class; **im**
  ersten Stock on the first floor
ertrinken to drown
erzählen to tell
es it; **es ist schön/warm** it's beautiful/
  warm
Essen food
essen to eat
etwas something; **etwas anderes**
  something else
euch you; **ein Freund von euch** a
  friend of yours *(see grammar)*
euer your *(see grammar)*

Euro euro
Europa Europe
Europäer, Europäerin European
europäisch European
Euroscheck Eurocheque

F

Fähre ferry
fahren to drive; to go
Fahrkarte ticket
Fahrkartenheft book of tickets
Fahrkartenschalter ticket office
Fahrplan timetable
Fahrpreis fare
Fahrrad bicycle
fallen to fall
falsch wrong
Familie family
fangen to catch
Farbe colour; paint
Fassbier draught beer
fast almost
Februar February
fehlen: mir fehlen zwei Euro I'm two
  euros short; **es fehlen drei ...** there are
  three ... missing
Fehler mistake; flaw; **einen Fehler**
  machen to make a mistake
Feinkostgeschäft deli
Felsen rock
Fenster window
Feriendorf holiday camp
Fernglas binoculars
Fernsehen television
fertig ready
fest tight; firm; strong
festsitzen: ich sitze fest I'm stuck
Fett fat
fettarm low-fat
feucht damp
Feuchtigkeitscreme moisturizer
Feuer fire; **haben Sie Feuer?** do you
  have a light?; **Feuer!** fire!

Feuerwehr fire brigade
Feuerwerk fireworks
Feuerzeug lighter
Fieber fever; **Fieber haben** to have a temperature; **bei jemandem Fieber messen** to take someone's temperature
finden to find
Fisch fish
Fischgeschäft fish shop
flach flat
Flasche bottle
Flaschenöffner bottle opener
Fleck stain, spot
Fliege fly
fliegen to fly
Flug flight
Fluggesellschaft airline
Flughafen airport
Flugticket plane ticket
Flugzeug plane
Fluss river
Flut high tide
Fön hairdrier
Form shape
Foto photo; **ein Foto (von ...) machen** to take a photo (of ...)
fotografieren: jemanden fotografieren to take someone's photo
Frage question; **eine Frage stellen** to ask a question
fragen to ask
Frankreich France
Französisch French
französisch French
Frau woman; wife; Mrs; Miss
Frauenarzt gynaecologist
frei free
freihalten: einen Platz freihalten to keep a seat
Freitag Friday
Fremdenführer guide
Freund friend; boyfriend
Freundin friend; girlfriend

Friedhof cemetery
Friseur, Friseurin hairdresser
früh early
früher former; earlier; formerly
Frühling spring
Frühstück breakfast
frühstücken to have breakfast
fühlen: sich fühlen to feel; **sich nicht wohl fühlen** to feel unwell; to feel uncomfortable
Führerschein driving licence
Führung guided tour
füllen to fill
Füller fountain pen
Füllung filling
für for; **für alle Fälle** just in case
furchtbar terrible
Fuß foot; **zu Fuß** on foot
Fußball football
Fußgänger pedestrian
Fußgängerzone pedestrian precinct

G

Gabel fork
Gallerie gallery
ganze whole; **den ganzen Tag** all day; **die ganze Woche** all week; **die ganze Zeit** all the time
Garantie guarantee
Garderobe cloakroom
Garten garden
Gaskartusche gas cylinder
Gast guest
Gaze gauze
Gebäude building
geben give; **es gibt ...** there is/are ...
gebraten fried; roast
gebraucht second-hand
gebrochen broken
Gebühr charge; toll
Geburtsdatum date of birth
Geburtstag birthday; date of birth
gefährlich dangerous

Gefallen favour; **jemandem einen Gefallen tun** to do someone a favour
Gefühl feeling
gegen against; **gegen vier Uhr** at about four o'clock
Gegend area; **in der Gegend** in the area; **hier/dort in der Gegend** around here/there
Gegenstand item
Gegenteil: das Gegenteil the opposite
gegenüber opposite; towards
gehen to go; to walk; **mir geht es gut/schlecht** I feel good/bad
gehören: es gehört mir/ihr it's mine/hers; **wem gehört das?** whose is it?
geimpft (gegen) vaccinated (against)
gekocht cooked
gelaunt: gut/schlecht gelaunt sein to be in a good/bad mood
gelb yellow
Geld money
Geldautomat cashpoint
Geldstrafe fine
Gelegenheit opportunity
Gemälde painting
genau exact; exactly; **genau hier** right here
genießen to enjoy
genug enough
geöffnet open
Gepäck luggage
Gepäckaufbewahrung left-luggage (office)
Gepäckwagen trolley
gerade just; **ich bin gerade angekommen** I've just arrived; **gerade eben** just now; **gerade tun wollen** be about to do
geradeaus straight ahead, straight on
Geräusch noise
Gericht dish; court
gern geschehen! don't mention it!, it's a pleasure!
Geruch smell
gesalzen salted

Geschäft shop
Geschäftsführer manager
Geschenk present
Geschenkpapier gift wrap
Geschirr dishes; **das Geschirr spülen** do the dishes
Geschirrspülmaschine dishwasher
Geschirrtuch dish towel
Geschlecht sex
geschlossen closed, shut
Geschmack taste; flavour
Geschwindigkeit speed
geschwollen swollen
gesetzlicher Feiertag public holiday
Gesicht face
gestern yesterday; **gestern Abend** yesterday evening
Gesundheit health; **Gesundheit!** bless you!
Getränk drink
getrennt separately
Getriebe gearbox
gewöhnt: ich bin das gewöhnt I'm used to it
Gewürz spice
Gipfel summit
Gips plaster (cast)
Glas glass; **ein Glas Wasser/Wein** a glass of water/wine
glauben to believe
gleiche same; **das Gleiche** the same
Gleis platform
Glück luck; **Glück haben** to be lucky
glücklich happy
Glühbirne light bulb
Golfplatz golf course
Grad degree
Gramm grams
Gras grass
grau grey
Grieche, Griechin Greek
Griechenland Greece
Griechisch Greek
griechisch Greek

Grill barbecue
Grillparty barbecue
Grippe flu
groß big; tall
Großbritannien Great Britain
Größe size
grün green
gültig valid
gut good; **guten Morgen** good
morning; **guten Tag** good afternoon;
guten Abend good evening; **gute
Nacht** goodnight; **guten Appetit!**
enjoy your meal!; **mir geht es gut**
I'm well

H

Haare hair
haben to have *(see grammar)*
Hafen harbour; port
halb half; **ein halber Liter** half a litre;
ein halbes Kilo half a kilo; **eine halbe
Stunde** half an hour
Halbpension half-board
hallo hello
Hals neck; throat
Halsschmerzen haben to have a sore
throat
Halt stop; **Halt machen** to stop
halten to hold; to last
Haltestelle stop
Hämorrhoiden piles
Handbremse handbrake
Handgelenk wrist
handgemacht hand-made
Handgepäck hand luggage
Handtasche handbag
Handtuch towel
Handy mobile (phone)
Hansaplast® Elastoplast®
hart hard
hassen to hate
Haupt- main; **Hauptgericht** main
course

Haus house; **zu Hause** at home; **nach
Hause gehen/fahren/fliegen** to go
home
Hausarbeit housework; **die Hausarbeit
machen** to do the housework
Haut skin
heben: die Hand heben to put up
one's hand
Heftpflaster sticking plaster
heiß hot; **es ist heiß** it's hot; **mir ist
heiß** I'm hot; **heißes Getränk** hot
drink
heiße Schokolade hot chocolate
heißen to be called; to mean; **ich heiße
...** my name is …
Heizung heating; radiator
helfen to help
hell light; **hellblau** light blue
Helm helmet
Hemd shirt
herauskommen to come out
Herbst autumn
hereinkommen to come in
Hering herring; tent peg
Herr gentleman; Mr
Herren(toilette) gents (toilet)
herrlich wonderful
Herz heart
Herzanfall heart attack
Heuschnupfen hay fever
heute today; **heute Abend** this evening;
heute Nacht tonight; **heute im
Angebot** today's special
heutzutage nowadays
hier here; **hier ist/sind ...** here is/are ...
Hi-Fi-Anlage hi-fi
Hilfe help; **um Hilfe rufen** call for help;
Hilfe! help!
Himmel sky
hinausgehen to go out
hinauswerfen to throw out
hineingehen to go in
Hinfahrt outward journey
Hinflug outward flight

hinsetzen: sich hinsetzen to sit down
hinten at the back; **hinten im Bus/ Buch** at the back of the bus/book
hinter behind
Hitze heat
hoch high; tall
Höchstgeschwindigkeit: mit Höchstgeschwindigkeit at full speed
Hochzeitsreise honeymoon
Hochzeitstag wedding anniversary
höhere Schule secondary school
holen to fetch, to get
Holz wood
homosexuell homosexual
hören to hear
Hose trousers
Hüfte hip
Hügel hill
Hunger hunger; **Hunger haben** to be hungry
Husten cough; **Husten haben** to have a cough
husten to cough
Hut hat

I

ich I; **ich bin Deutscher** I'm German; **ich bin 22 (Jahre alt)** I'm 22 (years old)
ihm (to) him/it; **ein Freund von ihm** a friend of his
ihn him/it
Ihnen (to) you; **wie geht es Ihnen** how are you? *(see grammar)*
ihnen (to) them; **ein Freund von ihnen** a friend of theirs
Ihr your *(see grammar)*
ihr you; (to) her/it; her/its/their; **ein Freund von ihr** a friend of hers *(see grammar)*
im in the; **im Zug/Flugzeug sitzen** be on the train/plane; **im 19. Jahrhundert** in the 19th century

Imbiss snack; snack bar
immer always
in in; **in England** in England; **in einer Stunde** in an hour
inbegriffen included
Infektion infection
Inliner rollerblades
Insekt insect
Insektengift insecticide
Insel island
Installateur plumber
internationale Zahlungsanweisung international money order
irgendwo somewhere; **irgendwo anders** somewhere else
Ire Irishman; **die Iren** the Irish
Irin Irishwoman
irisch Irish
Irland Ireland
Italien Italy
Italiener, Italienerin Italian
Italienisch Italian
italienisch Italian

J

ja yes
Jachthafen marina
Jacke jacket
Jahr year
Jahreszeit season
Jahrhundert century
Januar January
jeder, jede, jedes everyone; each (one), every (one)
jemand someone; anyone
jetzt now
Joggen jogging
jucken: es juckt it's itchy
Jugendherberge youth hostel
Juli July
jung young
Juni June
Juwelier jeweller's

Kaffee coffee
Kai quay
Kajak kayak
kalt cold; **es ist kalt** it's cold; **mir ist kalt** I'm cold
Kamera camera
Kamm comb
Kampf fight
Kanal channel
Kanne pot
Kapelle chapel
kaputt damaged
Karte card; map
Karussell roundabout
Kasse checkout; ticket office
Kassenbon receipt
Katastrophe disaster
Kater hangover
kaufen buy
Kaufhaus department store
Kaution deposit
kein, keine no, not ... any; **ich habe kein Geld** I haven't got any money; **keine Ahnung** no idea; **wir haben kein Benzin mehr** we've run out of petrol; **kein Trinkwasser** non-drinking water (see grammar)
keiner, keine, keines nobody; none
Kellner waiter
Kellnerin waitress
Kennzeichen registration number
Kerze candle
Kilo kilo(s)
Kilometer kilometre(s)
Kind child
Kinderwagen pram
Kinn chin
Kino cinema
Kirche church
Kirmes funfair
Klebeband Sellotape®
Kleiderbügel coathanger

klein small, little
klemmen: die Tür klemmt the door's stuck
Klettern climbing
Klima climate
Klimaanlage air conditioning
klingeln to ring
Klippe cliff
Kloster monastery
Knie knee
Knöchel ankle
kochen cook
Kochplatte hotplate
Kochtopf saucepan
Koffer suitcase
Kofferraum boot
Kohlensäure: mit Kohlensäure fizzy
komfortabel comfortable
kommen to come
Kondom condom
können can, to be able to; **ich kann nicht** I can't; **es könnte regnen** it might rain
Konsulat consulate
Kontakt contact; **in Kontakt bleiben** to stay in touch
kontaktieren to contact
Kontaktlinse contact lens
kontrollieren to check
Konzert concert
Konzerthalle concert hall
Kopf head
Kopfkissen pillow
Kopfkissenbezug pillowcase
Kopfschmerzen headache; **Kopfschmerzen haben** to have a headache
Kopfschmerztablette aspirin
Korkenzieher corkscrew
Körper body
Kosten cost
kosten to cost
Krach noise; **Krach machen** to make a noise

krank ill; **krank werden** to fall ill
Krankenhaus hospital
Krankenpfleger (male) nurse
Krankenschwester nurse
Krankenwagen ambulance
Krankheit illness
Krawatte tie
Kreditkarte credit card
Kreisverkehr roundabout
Kreuz cross
Krug jug
Küche kitchen
Kuchen cake; pie
Küchenschabe cockroach
Kugel: eine Kugel Eis a scoop of ice cream
Kugelschreiber (ballpoint) pen
kühl cool
Kühlschrank fridge
Kulturbeutel toilet bag
kümmern: sich kümmern um to look after
Kunst art
Künstler artist
Kunstwerk work of art
Kupplung clutch
kurz short
kurzärmelig short-sleeved
Küste coast

Lächeln smile
lächeln to smile
lachen to laugh
Ladenbesitzer, Ladenbesitzerin shopkeeper
Laken sheet
Lampe lamp
Land country; countryside
Landschaft countryside; landscape; scenery
lang long; **eine Stunde lang** for an hour
lange a long time; **wie lange?** how long?

langsam slow; slowly
lassen to let; to leave; **offen lassen** to leave open
Lastwagen lorry
laut loud; noisy
lauwarm lukewarm
Leben life
leben to live
lebendig alive; lively
Lebensmittelgeschäft grocer's
Lebensmittelvergiftung food poisoning
Leber liver
leer empty
legen to put; to lay
leicht light; easy
leiden to suffer
leihen to lend
lernen to learn
lesen to read
letzte last; **letztes Jahr** last year
Leuchtturm lighthouse
Leute people
Licht light
lieb dear; **Lieber Herr Brown** Dear Mr Brown; **Liebe Susanne** Dear Susanne
Liebe love
lieben to love
lieber mögen to prefer
Lieblings- favourite
Lied song
liegen to lie; **liegen lassen** to leave (behind)
lila purple
Linie line
linke left
links (von) to the left (of)
Linse lens; lentil
Lippe lip
Liter litre(s)
Löffel spoon
lohnen: es lohnt sich it's worth it
Luft air
Luftpost airmail
Luftpumpe bicycle pump

Lunchpaket packed lunch
Lunge lung
Luxemburg Luxembourg
Luxus luxury
Luxus- luxury

M

machen to make; to do; **das macht nichts** it doesn't matter
Mädchen girl
Mädchenname maiden name
Magen stomach
Mahlzeit meal
Mai May
man: man sagt ... they say that ...
manche some; **manche Leute** some people
manchmal sometimes
Mann man; husband
Markt market
März March
Matratze mattress
Maus mouse
Medikament medicine
Meer sea; **am Meer** at the seaside
Meeresblick sea view
Meeresfrüchte seafood
mehr more; **mehr als** more than; **viel mehr** much more, a lot more; **es gibt kein(e) ... mehr** there's no more ...
mehrere several
Mehrwertsteuer VAT
mein my (see grammar)
Meinung opinion; **meiner Meinung nach** in my opinion
meiste most; **am meisten** most; **die meisten** most; most people
Menü menu
Messe mass; fair
Messer knife
Meter metre(s)
Metzger butcher's
mich me; myself

Miete rent
mieten to rent; to hire
Mietwagen rental car
Mikrowelle microwave
Milchkaffee latte
mindeste least; **das Mindeste** the least
mindestens at least
Mineralwasser mineral water
Minute minute; **in letzter Minute** at the last minute
mir (to) me; **ein Freund von mir** a friend of mine
mit with; **mit dem Auto** by car
Mitglied member
mitnehmen: können Sie mich mitnehmen? can you give me a lift?
Mittag midday; **zu Mittag essen** have lunch
Mittagessen lunch
Mitte middle; **in der Mitte** in the middle
mitten: mitten in der Nacht in the middle of the night; **mitten auf der Straße** in the middle of the street
Mitternacht midnight
mittlere middle; medium
Mittwoch Wednesday
mögen like; **ich möchte ...** I'd like ...
möglich possible
Moment moment; **im Moment** at the moment
Monat month
Mond moon
Montag Monday
Morgen morning
morgen tomorrow; **morgen Abend** tomorrow evening; **morgen früh** tomorrow morning
Moschee mosque
Motor engine
Motorrad motorbike
Mücke mosquito
müde tired
Mühle mill

Müll rubbish; **den Müll hinausbringen** to take the rubbish out
Mülltonne dustbin
Mund mouth
Münze coin
Musik music
Muskel muscle
müssen to have to, must; **ich muss gehen** I have to go, I must go; **es muss drei Uhr sein** it must be three o'clock
Mutter mother
MwSt VAT

N

nach after; to; past; **nach England/London** to England/London; **Viertel nach zehn** a quarter past ten
Nachbar neighbour
nachdenken über to think about
Nachmittag afternoon
Nachname surname
Nachricht message
Nachrichten news
Nachspeise dessert
nächste next; nearest
Nacht night
Nachthemd nightdress
nackt naked
Nagel nail
nah near; **nah am Strand** near the beach
Nähe: in der Nähe nearby; **hier in der Nähe** round here
Name name
Narkose anaesthetic
Nase nose
nass wet
Nationalfeiertag national holiday
Natur nature
natürlich of course; natural
neben beside
nehmen take
nein no; **nein, danke** no, thank you

Nepp rip-off
nervös nervous
nett nice
neu new
Neujahr New Year
nicht not *(see grammar)*
Nichtraucher non-smoker
nichts nothing
Nickerchen nap; **ein Nickerchen machen** to have a nap
nie never
Niederlande: die Niederlande the Netherlands
niedrig low; **niedriger Blutdruck** low blood pressure
niemand no one, nobody
Niere kidney
nirgends nowhere
noch still; **noch ein** another; **noch einmal** again; **noch nicht** not yet
Norden north; **im Norden** in the north
nördlich von (to the) north of
normalerweise usually
Notausgang emergency exit
Notdienstapotheke out-of-hours pharmacist
Notfall emergency; **im Notfall** in an emergency
Notiz note
Notizbuch notebook
notwendig necessary
November November
null zero
Nummer number
nur only, just
nützlich useful
nutzlos useless

O

oben upstairs; at the top
Oberschenkel thigh
Oberteil top
obwohl although

oder or
Ofen oven
offen open
offensichtlich obvious
öffentlich public
Öffentlichkeit: die Öffentlichkeit the public
öffnen to open
oft often
ohne without; **ohne Gluten** gluten-free
ohnmächtig werden to faint
Ohnmachtsanfall blackout
Ohr ear
Ohropax® earplugs
Ohrringe earrings
Oktober October
Öl oil
operieren to operate on; **operiert werden** to have an operation
Optiker optician
Orchester orchestra
ordentlich tidy
ordnen to sort out; to arrange
organisieren to organize
Orientierungssinn: einen guten Orientierungssinn haben to have a good sense of direction
Ort place
Ortszeit local time
Osten east; **im Osten** in the east
Ostern Easter
östlich von (to the) east of

P

Paar pair; **ein Paar Shorts** a pair of shorts
paar: ein paar a few
Päckchen parcel
packen to pack
Packung packet
Paket parcel
Palast palace
Panne breakdown; **eine Panne haben** to break down

Pannendienst breakdown service
Papier paper
Papiertaschentuch paper tissue
Parfüm perfume
Park park
parken to park
Parkhaus multi-storey car park
Parkplatz car park; parking space
Parkuhr parking meter
Partei party
Pass passport; pass
Passagier passenger
passieren to happen
passen: passt Ihnen das? does that suit you?
Pastete pie; pâté
Patient, Patientin patient
Pauschalurlaub package holiday
Pause break, rest; interval
Pension guest house
perfekt perfect
Periode period
Personalausweis identity card
Pferd horse
Pflanze plant
Pfund pound
Pickel spot
Picknick picnic
picknicken to have a picnic
Pille pill; **die Pille nehmen** to be on the pill; **Pille danach** morning-after pill
pinkeln to pee
Pinsel brush
Plakat poster
planen to plan
Plastik plastic
Plastiktüte plastic bag
platt flat
Platz seat; space; place; square
platzen to burst
PLZ postcode
Polizei police
Polizeirevier police station
Polizist policeman

Polizistin policewoman
Portmonnaie purse
Porträt portrait
Portugiese, Portugiesin Portuguese
Portugiesisch Portuguese
portugiesisch Portuguese
Portwein port
Post post; post office
Postkarte postcard
postlagernd poste restante
Postleitzahl postcode
praktisch practical
Preis price; prize
privat private
probieren to try
Produkt product
Programm programme
Prospekt brochure, leaflet
prost! cheers!
Prozent percent
Prozession procession
Puder powder
Pulli jumper, sweater
Pulverkaffee instant coffee
Punkt point
pünktlich on time
putzen to clean
Pyjama pyjamas

Qualität quality; **von guter/schlechter Qualität** of good/bad quality
Quittung receipt

R

Rabatt discount; **jemandem Rabatt gewähren** to give someone a discount
Rad wheel; bike
Radiosender radio station
Radweg cycle path
Rasierapparat razor; shaver
Rasiercreme shaving cream

rasieren: sich rasieren to shave
Rasierklinge razor blade
Rasierschaum shaving foam
Rassist, Rassistin racist
Rat advice; **jemanden um Rat fragen** to ask someone's advice
raten to advise
Rauch smoke
rauchen to smoke
Raucher, Raucherin smoker
Rechnung bill
Recht right
rechte right
rechts (von) to the right (of)
reduzieren to reduce
Reduzierung reduction
Regen rain
Regenmantel raincoat
Regenschirm umbrella
regnen to rain; **es regnet** it's raining
reichen to be enough; **das reicht** that's enough
reif ripe
Reifen tyre
Reise journey; trip; **gute Reise!** have a good trip!
Reisebüro travel agent's
Reiseführer guidebook; guide
reisen to travel
Reisescheck traveller's cheque
Reisezentrum ticket office
Reißverschluss zip
reparieren to repair; **etwas reparieren lassen** to get something repaired
Reserverad spare wheel
Reservereifen spare tyre
reservieren to reserve, to book
reserviert reserved
retten to save
Rezept prescription; recipe
Rezeption reception; **an der Rezeption** at reception
R-Gespräch reverse-charge call
Rheuma rheumatism

richtig correct, right
Richtung direction
riechen to smell; **gut/schlecht riechen** to smell good/bad
Rippe rib
Risiko risk
Rock skirt
roh raw
Rohr pipe
Roller scooter
Rollstuhl wheelchair
Roman novel
Röntgen X-rays
rosa pink
rot red; **rote Ampel** red light
Rotwein red wine
Rücken back
Rückfahrkarte return (ticket)
Rückkehr return
Rückwärtsgang reverse gear
ruhig quiet; calm
Ruinen ruins
rund round
Rundfahrt tour; cruise
Rutsche slide

S

Saft juice
sagen to say; to tell
Saison season
Salbe ointment
Salz salt
salzig salty
Sammlung collection
Samstag Saturday
Sandalen sandals
Sänger, Sängerin singer
satt haben to be fed up with
Satz sentence
sauber clean; **sauber machen** to clean
Schachtel packet
schade what a shame

schaffen to manage; **es schaffen, etwas zu tun** to manage to do something
schälen to peel
Schatten shade; **im Schatten** in the shade
Schauer shower
Schaufenster (shop) window; **im Schaufenster** in the window
Scheck cheque
Scheibe slice; **in Scheiben** sliced
Schein banknote
scheinen to seem; **es scheint ...** it seems that ...
Scheinwerfer headlight
Schere scissors
schicken to send
schieben to push
Schiff boat
Schild sign
Schlaf sleep
schlafen to sleep; **schlafen mit** to sleep with
Schlaflosigkeit insomnia
Schlafsack sleeping bag
Schlaftablette sleeping pill
Schlag (electric) shock; blow
Schläger racket; club
Schlange queue; snake; **Schlange stehen** queue
schlecht bad; sick; **mir ist schlecht** I feel sick
schlechter worse; **schlechter werden** to get worse; **es ist schlechter (als)** it's worse (than)
Schlepplift T-bar
schließen to close, to shut
Schloss lock; castle
Schlüssel key
schmecken to taste; **schmecken nach** to taste of; **hat es geschmeckt?** did you enjoy that?
Schmuck jewellery
schmutzig dirty

Schnee snow
schneiden to cut; **sich schneiden** to cut oneself
schneien to snow; **es schneit** it's snowing
schnell fast; quickly
Schock shock
schon already
schön beautiful; good
Schornstein chimney
Schotte, Schottin Scot
schottisch Scottish
Schottland Scotland
Schrei shout; cry
schreiben to write; **wie schreibt man ...?** how do you spell ...?
schreien to shout; to cry
Schritt step
schüchtern shy
Schuhe shoes
schulden to owe
Schulter shoulder
Schüssel bowl
schützen to protect
schwach weak
Schwamm sponge
schwanger pregnant
schwarz black
schwer heavy; difficult
Schwester sister
schwierig difficult
Schwierigkeit: in Schwierigkeiten stecken to be in trouble
Schwimmbad swimming pool
schwimmen to swim; **schwimmen gehen** to go for a swim
schwitzen to sweat
schwul gay
See lake; sea
seekrank seasick
Segel sail
segeln to sail; **segeln gehen** to go sailing
sehen to see
sehr very

Seife soap
sein to be *(see grammar)*
sein his; **seine Schuhe** his shoes *(see grammar)*
seit since
Seite side; page
Sekunde second
selbst: (er) selbst himself; **(ich) selbst** myself; **(wir) selbst** ourselves
Selbstbewusstsein self-confidence
selten rare; rarely
seltsam strange
Sender station
September September
Serviette napkin
Sessellift chairlift
sich himself; herself; themselves; yourself; **sie kennen sich** they know each other
sicher safe; sure
Sicherheit safety; security
Sicherheitsgurt safety belt
Sicherung fuse
Sie you *(see grammar)*
sie she/it; her/it; they; them
Silber silver
singen to sing
Sinn sense; **Sinn haben** to make sense
Sirup syrup
Skier skis
skifahren gehen to go skiing
Skilift ski lift
Skiort ski resort
Skistiefel ski boots
Skistock ski pole
so so; like this
sobald as soon as
Socken socks
sodass so that
sofort right away
Sohn son
Sommer summer
Sonne sun; **in der Sonne** in the sun
sonnen: sich sonnen to sunbathe
Sonnenaufgang sunrise

Sonnenbrand: einen Sonnenbrand bekommen to get sunburnt
Sonnenbrille sunglasses
Sonnencreme sun cream
Sonnenhut sunhat
Sonnenschirm beach umbrella
Sonnenstich sunstroke; **einen Sonnenstich bekommen** to get sunstroke
Sonnenuntergang sunset
Sonntag Sunday
sonst otherwise
sowie as well as
sowieso anyway
Spanien Spain
Spanier, Spanierin Spaniard
Spanisch Spanish
spanisch Spanish
sparen to save
spät late
spazieren: spazieren gehen to go for a walk; **spazieren fahren** to go for a drive
speichern to save
Speisekarte menu
Spezialität speciality
speziell special
Spiegel mirror
Spiel game, match
spielen to play
Spielzeug toy
Spinne spider
Spirale coil; spiral
Spitze point; tip
Splitter splinter
sportlich sporty
Sportplatz sports ground
Sporttauchen scuba diving
Sprache language
sprechen to speak, to talk
Spritze injection
Spülmittel washing-up liquid
Staat state
Stadion stadium

Stadt city; town
Stadthalle town hall
Stadtplan street map
Stadtzentrum city centre; town centre
stammen aus to come from; to date from
stark strong
starten to take off
stattdessen instead
Stau traffic jam
stechen to sting; **gestochen werden (von)** to get stung (by)
Steckdose socket
stecken to put
Stecker plug
stehlen to steal
Stein stone; rock
Stelle job; place
stellen to put
sterben to die
Steuer tax
steuerfrei tax-free
Stich sting
Stiefel boot
Stil style
still silent; still; **stilles Wasser** still water
Stirn forehead
Stock floor, storey; stick
stolz (auf) proud (of)
Stöpsel plug
stören to disturb; **bitte nicht stören** do not disturb
Stoßstange bumper
Strand beach
Straße road; street
Straßenbahn tram
Streichholz match
Streit argument
Strom electricity
Stromausfall blackout
Stromzähler electricity meter
Strumpfhose tights
Stück piece; play; **ein Stück ...** a piece of ...; **ein Stück Obst** a piece of fruit

Student, Studentin student
studieren to study
Studium studies
Stufe step; stage
Stuhl chair
Stunde hour; **eineinhalb Stunden** an hour and a half
Sturm storm
suchen to look for
Süden south; **im Süden** in the south
südlich von (to the) south of
Supermarkt supermarket
Surfbrett surfboard
surfen to surf; **surfen gehen** to go surfing
süß sweet
Süßigkeit sweet
Synagoge synagogue

T

Tabak tobacco
Tabakgeschäft tobacconist's
Tablette tablet
Tag day
Tagesgericht dish of the day
täglich every day
Taille waist
Tal valley
Tankstelle petrol station
Tanz dance
tanzen to dance
Tasche bag
Taschenlampe torch
Taschentuch handkerchief
Tasse cup
Tatsache fact
tatsächlich really
taub deaf
tauchen gehen to go diving
Taucheranzug wetsuit
Taxameter meter
Taxifahrer, Taxifahrerin taxi driver
Teelöffel teaspoon

Teil part
teilen to share
Telefon phone
Telefonbuch telephone directory
Telefonist, Telefonistin switchboard operator
Telefonkarte phonecard
Telefonnummer phone number
Telefonzelle phone box
Teller plate
Temperatur temperature
Tennisplatz tennis court
Tennisschuhe tennis shoes
Teppich carpet; rug
Termin appointment; **einen Termin vereinbaren** to make an appointment; **einen Termin haben (mit)** to have an appointment (with)
Terrasse patio
teuer expensive
Theater theatre
Thermosflasche Thermos® flask
tief deep
Tiefkühltruhe freezer
Tier animal
Tipp tip
tippen to type
Tisch table
Tochter daughter
Toilette toilet
Toilettenartikel toiletries
Toilettenpapier toilet paper
toll great
Topf pot
Tor gate; goal
tot dead
töten to kill
Touristenfalle tourist trap
Touristeninformation tourist office
Touristenklasse economy class
traditionell traditional
tragen to carry; to wear
trampen to hitchhike
traurig sad

Treffen meeting
treffen to meet
trennen to separate; **sich trennen** to split up
Treppe stairs
trinken drink; **etwas trinken** to have a drink; **etwas trinken gehen** to go for a drink
Trinkgeld tip
Trinkwasser drinking water
trocken dry
Trockenreinigung dry cleaner's
trocknen to dry
Tropfen drops
trotzdem all the same
tschüss! bye!
tun to do
Tür door
typisch typical

U

U-Bahn underground
U-Bahn-Linie underground line
U-Bahn-Station underground station
über above; over; about
überall everywhere
überallhin everywhere
überfallen to attack
Übergewicht: mein Gepäck hat Übergewicht my luggage is overweight
überhaupt nicht not at all
überholen to overtake, to pass
übermorgen the day after tomorrow
übernachten to stay
überqueren to cross
überraschen to surprise
Überraschung surprise
übersetzen to translate
übertrieben overdone
Überweisung transfer
Uhr watch; clock; o'clock; **drei Uhr** three o'clock; **wie viel Uhr ist es?** what time is it?

um around; by; **um eine Uhr** at one o'clock; **um ... herum** around
Umkleide changing room; fitting room
Umschlag envelope
umso besser all the better
umtauschen to exchange
Umzug procession
unabhängig independent
unbequem uncomfortable
und and
undicht sein to leak
Unfall accident
ungefähr about
uns us; **ein Freund von uns** a friend of ours
unser our *(see grammar)*
Unsinn nonsense
unten downstairs; at the bottom
unter under; below; among; **unter der Woche** during the week
Unterhose underpants
Unterkunft accommodation
Unternehmen company
unterschreiben to sign
Unterschrift signature
Untertitel: mit Untertiteln subtitled
Unterwäsche underwear
unverheiratet single
Urlaub holiday(s); **Urlaub machen** to be on holiday

V

Vater father
Vegetarier, Vegetarierin vegetarian
vegetarisch vegetarian
Ventilator fan
verabreden: sich verabreden to arrange to meet
Veranstaltungskalender listings magazine
Verband bandage
Verbindung connection
verbleites Benzin four-star petrol

verboten forbidden
verbraten overdone
verbrennen: sich verbrennen to burn oneself
Verbrennung burn
verbringen to spend
verderben to spoil
Vereinigte Staaten: die Vereinigten Staaten the United States
verfügbar available
vergewaltigen to rape
Vergewaltigung rape
Vergnügen pleasure
Vergnügungspark theme park
verheiratet married
Verhütungsmittel contraceptive
Verkauf sale
verkaufen to sell; **zu verkaufen** for sale
Verkäufer, Verkäuferin shop assistant
Verkehr traffic
verkocht overdone
verlassen to leave
verlaufen: sich verlaufen to get lost; **sich verlaufen haben** to be lost
verletzt injured
verlieben: sich verlieben to fall in love
verlieren to lose
verlobt engaged
Verlobte fiancé; fiancée
vermieten to let (out); to rent (out)
vermissen to miss
vernünftig reasonable
verpassen to miss
Verpflegung board
Versicherung insurance
versilbert silver-plated
verspätet delayed
Verspätung to delay
versprechen to promise
verstauchen: sich den Knöchel verstauchen to sprain one's ankle
verstehen to understand
Verstopfung haben to be constipated

versuchen to try; **versuchen, etwas zu tun** to try to do something
verwöhnen to spoil
viel, viele a lot (of)
vielleicht perhaps
Viertel quarter; **Viertel vor zehn** a quarter to ten
Viertelstunde quarter of an hour
Visum visa
Volk people
voll full; **voller Preis** full price; full fare; **voll tanken** to fill up with petrol
voller full of
Vollkaskoversicherung comprehensive insurance
Vollpension full board
von from; of; by; **von ... nach ...** from … to …
vor before; in front of; **vor zehn Jahren** ten years ago
vorbeifahren to pass
vorbeigehen to pass
vorbereiten to prepare
vorbestellen to reserve, to book
Vorderseite front
vorgestern the day before yesterday
vorher in advance
Vorhersage forecast
Vorname first name
vorne at the front
Vorort suburb
vorrätig: nicht vorrätig out of stock
vorschlagen to suggest, to propose
vorübergehend temporary
Vorwahl dialling code
vorwärts forward

W

wachsen to grow
wahr true
während while; during
wahrscheinlich probably
Währung currency

Wahrzeichen landmark
Wald forest; wood
Waliser Welshman
Waliserin Welshwoman
walisisch Welsh
Walkman® personal stereo, Walkman®
wandern gehen to go hiking
Wanderschuhe walking boots
wann when
Waren goods
warnen warn
warten to wait; **auf jemanden/etwas warten** to wait for someone/something
warum why
was what; **was wollen Sie?** what do you want?; **was für ein(e) ...?** what kind of ...?
Waschbecken washbasin
Wäsche waschen to do the washing
waschen to wash; **sich waschen** to have a wash; **sich die Haare waschen** to wash one's hair
Waschlappen facecloth
Waschmaschine washing machine
Waschpulver washing powder
Waschsalon launderette
Wasser water
wasserdicht waterproof
Wasserhahn tap
Wasserski waterskiing
Watte cotton wool
Wattestäbchen cotton bud
Wechsel change
Wechselgeld change
Wechselkurs exchange rate
wechseln to change
Wecker alarm clock
weder ... noch ... neither ... nor ...
Weg path; way
weg away
wegen because of
wegfahren to drive away; to go away
wegfliegen to fly off; to go away
weggehen to go away

wehtun to hurt; **mein Kopf tut weh** my head hurts
weil because
Weile: eine Weile a while
Wein wine
weinen to cry
weiß white
Weißwein white wine
weit far; **weit von** far from
welcher, welche, welches which
Welle wave
Welt world
wenden to turn (round)
wenig: ein wenig a little
wenige few
weniger less; **weniger als** less than
wenigste least
wenn if; when
wer who
werden to become; to get; will; to be *(see grammar)*
werfen to throw
Werk work
Werkstatt garage
wert worth; **es ist keine 50 Euro wert** it's not worth 50 euros
Wespe wasp
wessen whose
Westen west; **im Westen** in the west
westlich von (to the) west of
Wetter weather
Wettervorhersage weather forecast
wichtig important
wie how; like; as; **wie geht es Ihnen?** how are you?; **wie viel kostet das?** how much is it?, how much does it cost?; **wie viele?** how many?; **wie oft?** how many times?; **so bald wie möglich** as soon as possible; **wie bitte?** pardon?
wiederholen to repeat
Wiedersehen: auf Wiedersehen goodbye
willkommen welcome
Windel nappy

Windschutzscheibe windscreen
Windsurfen windsurfing
wir we
wissen to know; **ich weiß nicht** I don't know
wo where; **wo ist/sind ...?** where is/are …?
Woche week
Wochenende weekend
woher: woher kommen Sie? where are you from?
wohin: wohin gehen Sie? where are you going?
Wohnmobil camper
Wohnung flat
Wohnwagen caravan
Wohnzimmer living room
Wolkenkratzer skyscraper
Wolle wool
wollen to want; **etwas tun wollen** to want to do something
Wunde wound
würzig spicy

Z

Zahl number
zählen to count
Zahn tooth
Zahnarzt dentist
Zahnbürste toothbrush
Zahnpasta toothpaste
Zeichen sign
zeigen to show
Zeit time; **von Zeit zu Zeit** from time to time
Zeitschrift magazine
Zeitung newspaper
Zeitungskiosk newsstand
Zeitungsladen newsagent's
Zeitunterschied time difference
Zelt tent
Zeltboden ground sheet

Zentimeter centimetre(s)
Zentrum centre
zerbrechlich fragile
zerstören to destroy
ziehen to pull
ziemlich quite; **ziemlich viel(e)** quite a lot of
Zigarette cigarette
Zigarettenpapier cigarette paper
Zigarre cigar
Zimmer room
Zirkus circus
Zoll customs
Zoomobjektiv zoom (lens)
zu to; towards; too; **zu klein** too small; **zu viele** too many; **zu viel** too much
zubereiten to prepare
zuerst first (of all)
Zug train; **der Zug nach München** the train to Munich
Zuhause home
zuhören to listen
zumindest at least
Zündkerze spark plug
Zunge tongue
zurückbekommen: sein Geld zurückbekommen to get a refund
zurückgeben to give back
zurückkehren to return
zurückkommen to come back
zurückrufen to call back
zusammen together
zusammenbrechen to break down
Zusammenbruch breakdown
zusätzlich extra
Zuschlag supplement
Zustand state
zwecklos pointless
zweimal twice
zweite second; **zweite Klasse** second class
zwischen between

GRAMMAR

Each German noun has one of three **genders**: masculine, feminine or neuter. These genders are indicated in the **definite article** (= the) and the **indefinite article** (= a) as follows:

	definite article	indefinite article
masculine	**der**	**ein**
feminine	**die**	**eine**
neuter	**das**	**ein**

The plural of the definite article, **die**, is the same for all genders. As in English, there is no plural form for the indefinite article:

die Kinder   the children   **Kinder**   children

These are the basic forms. However, unlike in English, a German noun changes its form according to the function of the noun within the sentence (its **case**). There are four cases in German:

The **nominative** case, used for the subject of the sentence:
> **der Zug** fährt ab   the train is departing

The **accusative** case, used for the direct object (directly affected by the action of the verb):
> kennst du **den Sänger?**   do you know the singer?

The **dative** case, used for the indirect object (to whom/which something is given or for whom/which something is done):
> geben Sie den Schlüssel **der Nachbarin**   give the key to the neighbour

The **genitive** case, used to show possession or association:
> der Anfang **des Liedes**   the beginning of the song

Cases for the definite article:

	nominative	accusative	dative	genitive
masculine	**der**	**den**	**dem**	**des** (+ **s** at end of noun)
feminine	**die**	**die**	**der**	**der**
neuter	**das**	**das**	**dem**	**des** (+ **s** at end of noun)
plural	**die**	**die**	**den** (+ **n** at end of noun)	**der**

Cases for the indefinite article:

	nominative	accusative	dative	genitive
masculine	ein	einen	einem	eines (+ **(e)s** at end of noun)
feminine	eine	eine	einer	einer
neuter	ein	ein	einem	eines (+ **(e)s** at end of noun)

Sometimes a case expresses a different function; for example, the accusative can be used to indicate the place to which you are going, and the dative can indicate the place where you are. Certain prepositions take only the accusative case, while others take only the dative or the genitive.

All **nouns** in German are written with a capital first letter.

In general, the gender of a noun representing a person corresponds to the sex of that person: **der Mann** the man; **die Frau** the woman.

Nouns ending in **-chen** or **-lein** are neuter.

Nouns ending in **-ei**, **-in**, **-ion**, **-heit**, **-keit**, **-schaft**, **-ung** and **-tät** are feminine.

The **plural** form of nouns differs from the singular form. Although there are many exceptions, the following guidelines are useful:

The plural ending of masculine nouns is typically an added **-e** (and sometimes the **a**, **o**, or **u** in the word becomes **ä**, **ö**, or **ü**). Sometimes the ending is **-er** or **-en**:

      der Freund the friend → **die Freunde** the friends
      der Mann the man → **die Männer** the men

The plural ending of feminine nouns is typically **-en**. Some plural feminine nouns end in **-e**, with the **a**, **o**, or **u** in the word becoming **ä**, **ö**, or **ü**:

      die Frau the woman → **die Frauen** the women
      die Nacht the night → **die Nächte** the nights

The plural ending of neuter nouns is typically **-er**, with the **a**, **o**, or **u** in the word becoming **ä**, **ö**, or **ü**:

      das Kind the child → **die Kinder** the children
      das Glas the glass → **die Gläser** the glasses

Some plural neuter nouns end in **-e**:

      das Jahr the year → **die Jahre** the years

As in English, German nouns can be put together to form longer **compound nouns**:

> **der Sommer** the summer + **die Ferien** the holidays = **die Sommerferien** the summer holidays

Sometimes the individual nouns are joined by **-(e)s-**:

> **das Frühstück** the breakfast + **das Fernsehen** the television = **das Frühstücksfernsehen** breakfast television

Adjectives do not vary with gender. However, if an adjective comes directly in front of a noun it alters its form depending on (1) whether it follows a definite or an indefinite article, and (2) the case of the noun:

	nominative	accusative	dative	genitive
masculine	**der** jung**e** Mann	**den/einen** jung**en** Mann	**dem/einem** jung**en** Mann	**des/eines** jung**en** Mannes
	ein jung**er** Mann			
feminine	**die/eine** jung**e** Frau	**die/eine** jung**e** Frau	**der/einer** jung**en** Frau	**der/einer** jung**en** Frau
neuter	**das** jung**e** Kind	**das** jung**e** Kind	**dem/einem** jung**en** Kind	**des/eines** jung**en** Kindes
	ein jung**es** Kind	**ein** jung**es** Kind		
plural	**die** jung**en** Frauen	**die** jung**en** Frauen	**den** jung**en** Frauen	**der** jung**en** Frauen
	jung**e** Frauen	jung**e** Frauen	jung**en** Frauen	jung**er** Frauen

If the adjective follows the noun to which it refers, then it does not change its form:

> **der Mann/das Kind ist groß** the man/child is tall
> **die Frau ist schön** the woman is beautiful

An **adverb** usually has the same form as the adjective:

> **der Mann ist freundlich** the man is friendly
> **der Mann spricht freundlich** the man speaks in a friendly way

The German word for the **demonstrative adjective** (= **this**, **these**, **that**, **those**) has the following basic forms:

masculine	feminine	neuter	plural
dieser	**diese**	**dieses**	**diese**

and takes the same case endings as the definite article **der**, **die**, **das**:

> **ich sehe den Mann** I see the man
> **ich sehe diesen Mann** I see this/that man

The German words for the **possessive adjectives** (= **my**, **your** etc) have the following basic forms:

	my	your (du/ihr/Sie)*	his	her	our	their
masculine	mein	dein/euer/Ihr	sein	ihr	unser	ihr
feminine	meine	deine/euere/Ihre	seine	ihre	unsere	ihre
neuter	mein	dein/euer/Ihr	sein	ihr	unser	ihr
plural	meine	deine/euere/Ihre	seine	ihre	unsere	ihre

(*See the Everyday Conversation chapter for the difference between **du**, **ihr** and **Sie**.)

They take the same case endings as the indefinite article **ein**, **eine**, **ein**:

> **ich sehe ein Kind** I see a child
> **ich sehe dein Kind** I see your child

The German words for the **personal pronouns** (= **I**, **you** etc) have the following basic forms:

I	you*	he	she	we	they
ich	du/ihr/Sie	er	sie	wir	ihr

and they have different forms according to their case:

nominative	ich	du/ihr/Sie	er	sie	wir	ihr
accusative	mich	dich/euch/Sie	ihn	sie	uns	sie
dative	mir	dir/euch/Ihnen	ihm	ihr	uns	ihnen

(*See the Everyday Conversation chapter for the difference between **du**, **ihr** and **Sie**.)

The infinitive (basic form) of German **verbs** is composed of a root plus **-(e)n**. For example: **haben** to have, **sein** to be, **gehen** to go. The endings that are added to the root depend on two factors: tense (time) and person (subject of the verb). There are two types of verbs: regular verbs, whose root never changes, and irregular verbs, whose root changes as tense and person change.

In the **present tense**, the verbs **haben** (to have) and **sein** (to be) have special forms which need to be learnt by heart:

> **haben**   **sein**
> ich habe   ich bin

du hast	du bist
er/sie hat	er/sie ist
wir haben	wir sind
ihr habt	ihr seid
sie haben	sie sind

Regular verbs have the following forms:

machen (to do, to make)

ich mach**e**	wir mach**en**
du mach**st**	ihr mach**t**
er/sie mach**t**	sie mach**en**

If the root ends in a **d**, in a **t** or in a consonant followed by **m** or **n**, then an **-e-** is added in the **du**, **er/sie** and **ihr** forms. For example, **arbeiten** (to work): **er arbeitet** (he works).

Irregular verbs take the same endings as regular verbs in the present tense, but many of them change the vowel in the **du** and **er/sie** forms:
Root in **-e-** → **-i-**
    sprechen (to speak, to talk) → ich spreche, du sprichst, er spricht ...
Root in **-a-** or **-au-** → **-ä-** or **-äu-**
    tragen (to carry, to wear) → ich trage, du trägst, er trägt ...
    laufen (to walk, to run) → ich laufe, du läufst, er läuft ...

As in English, the **perfect tense** in German is made up of an auxiliary verb (**haben** or **sein**; in English **have** is used) in the present tense and a past participle (in English the past participle is, for example, the word **done** in the sentence "she has done it"). The German past participle is either regular or irregular depending on the verb being used.

The past participle of regular verbs has the form: **ge-** + root + **-t**:
    machen (to do, to make) → **gemacht** (done, made)
    arbeiten (to work) → **gearbeitet** (worked)

The past participle of verbs of foreign origin and of verbs beginning with **be-**, **emp-**, **ent-**, **er-**, **ge-**, **ver-** and **zer-** do not add **ge-** to the root:
    reparieren (to repair) → **repariert** (repaired)
    bezahlen (to pay) → **bezahlt** (paid)

The past participle of irregular verbs has the form: **ge-** + root (perhaps altered) + **-en**:

sprechen (to speak, to talk) → **gesprochen** (spoken, talked)
lesen (to read) → **gelesen** (read)

The past participle of **sein** (be) is very irregular: **gewesen** (been).

Verbs which express a change of state or a change of place use **sein** as their auxiliary verb:

wachsen (to grow) → **ich bin gewachsen** (I've grown)
laufen (to walk, to run) → **ich bin gelaufen** (I've walked/run)

All other verbs use haben, with the exception of **sein** (to be): **ich bin gewesen** (I have been); and **bleiben** (to stay): **ich bin geblieben** (I have stayed).

In German, the perfect tense is also used to express the **simple past**, where in English the auxiliary would not be used. Thus, **ich habe gearbeitet** can mean both "I have worked" and "I worked", depending on the context.

The **imperfect tense** (used to express continuous action in the past; in English this usually takes the form: **was/were** + **-ing**) of regular verbs is formed as follows:

ich machte (I was doing/making)	**wir machten**
du machtest	**ihr machtet**
er/sie machte	**sie machten**

Irregular verbs have the following forms:

sprechen (to speak, to talk)

ich sprach (I was speaking/talking)	**wir sprachen**
du sprachst	**ihr sprachet**
er sprach	**sie sprachen**

Here are some common imperfect forms:

ich war I was	**ich dachte** I was thinking
ich hatte I had	**ich wusste** I knew
ich kam I was coming	**ich wollte** I wanted
ich ging I was going	**ich musste** I had to

In German, the **future tense** is regular for all verbs. The auxiliary verb **werden** (used on its own it means "to become") is followed by the infinitive (basic form) of the verb:

machen (to do, to make) → **ich werde machen** (I'll do/make)
sprechen (to speak, to talk) → **ich werde sprechen** (I'll speak/ talk)

The auxiliary verb **werden** has the following forms:

ich werde	wir werden
du wirst	ihr werdet
er/sie wird	sie werden

The basic way of expressing a **negative** idea in German is to use **nicht** (not). In a simple sentence (with just one clause), **nicht** comes after the verb:

ich weiß → I know   ich weiß nicht → I don't know

Nicht is also used in the negative expressions **noch nicht** (not yet) and **nicht mehr** (not any longer).

The word **kein** (not a/not any/no) is used before indefinite nouns (a/some). It has the same endings as **ein**:

ich habe einen Garten (I have a garden) → **ich habe keinen Garten** (I don't have a garden)
sie haben Kinder (they have children) → **sie haben keine Kinder** (they don't have any children)

German **word order** in a sentence is often different from English word order. There are a few basic rules:

In a simple sentence that is making a statement, the verb is always in second place. The subject often comes at the beginning of the sentence, but it can also come after the verb:

Peter kommt heute = heute kommt Peter
Peter is coming today

The infinitive and the past participle always come at the end:

Peter wird morgen kommen Peter will come tomorrow
Peter ist gestern gekommen Peter came yesterday

In a simple question, the verb comes first, as in English:

kommt Peter heute? is Peter coming today?

If the question includes interrogative adverbs such as **warum, wann, wer** etc (why, when, who etc), the word order is again the same as in English:

warum kommt Peter heute? why is Peter coming today?

HOLIDAYS AND FESTIVALS

BANK HOLIDAYS

Below is a list of German bank holidays. Note that not all of them are national; some are only holidays in particular **Länder** (administrative districts) or regions.

1 January	New Year's Day (**Neujahr**)
6 January	Epiphany (**Dreikönigstag**)
March/April	Good Friday (**Karfreitag**) Easter Sunday (**Ostersonntag**) Easter Monday (**Ostermontag**)
1 May	Labour Day (**Maifeiertag**)
May	Ascension (**Christi Himmelfahrt**) Whit Sunday (**Pfingstsonntag**) Whit Monday (**Pfingstmontag**)
May/June	Corpus Christi (**Fronleichnam**)
15 August	Assumption (**Mariae Himmelfahrt**)
3 October	Day of German Unity, commemorating the reunification of Germany (**Tag der deutschen Einheit**)
1 November	All Saints' Day (**Allerheiligen**)
25 December	Christmas (**1. Weihnachtstag**)
26 December	Christmas (**2. Weihnachtstag**)

Christmas Eve and New Year's Eve are effectively "half-day" holidays, since most shops close at midday and many people only work in the morning.

FESTIVALS AND CELEBRATIONS

Germany is a country of festivals (**Festspiele**). Each **Land** has its own cultural scene, and many local popular traditions remain alive and well, with numerous events taking place throughout the year. Here are some of the most important ones:

January/February	Carnival (**Karneval** in the Rheinland, **Fasching** in Bavaria and **Fastnacht** or **Fasnacht** in south-western Germany). Street parties and cultural events are organized in many towns, with the biggest in Cologne, Düsseldorf, Mainz and Munich. During the carnival procession (**Umzug**), decorated floats pass through the streets and locals in fancy dress hand out sweets to passers-by. Brass bands play and stalls selling sausages and beer stay open late into the night Berlin International Film Festival
March	**Frühlingsdom** (spring festival) in Hamburg. Other spring celebrations (**Frühlingsfeste**) are organized in various regions. Dresden Opera Festival Thuringia Bach Festival
April	Stuttgart Jazz Festival Berlin Music Festival
May	Red Wine Festival in Rüdesheim Dresden International Dixieland Jazz Festival Bonn Summer Festival (until September)
June	Munich Film Festival Various classical music festivals
July	Bayreuth Wagner Festival Music festival in Schleswig-Holstein Various local festivals throughout the country

August	Various wine festivals in the Rhineland Nuremberg Autumn Festival
September/October	**Oktoberfest** in Munich (world famous Bavarian beer festival, running from mid-September to the first Sunday in October). Long tables and tents are set up on the **Wies'n**, a large festival site, and the beer flows freely. Brass bands play and competitions are held to see who can drink the most beer. Leipzig Jazz Festival
November	Saint Martin's Festival in the Rhineland and Bavaria
December	Christmas festivities take place throughout December. Christmas markets (**Weihnachtsmärkte**) spring up in many cities. The best-known are held in Munich, Nuremberg, Berlin, Lübeck, Münster, Stuttgart and Heidelberg. Small wooden chalets are set up as market stalls, selling handicrafts which make good presents. Sausages and **Glühwein** (mulled wine) are available all day long to keep you warm.

USEFUL ADDRESSES

In the UK

**The German National
Tourist Office**
PO Box 2695
London W1A 3TN
Tel: 020 7824 1300
Fax: 020 7317 0917
e-mail: gntolon@d-z-t.com
www.germany-tourism.co.uk

The German Embassy
23 Belgrave Square
London SW1X 8PZ
Tel: 020 7317 0908
Fax: 020 7824 1449
e-mail: consular@german-embassy.
org.uk
www.german-embassy.org.uk

**The Austrian National
Tourist Office**
9-11 Richmond Buildings
(off Dean Street)
London W1D 3HF
Tel: 0845 101 1818
Fax: 0845 101 1819
e-mail: holiday@austria.info
www.austria-tourism.at/uk

The Austrian Embassy
18 Belgrave Mews West
London SW1X 8HU
Tel: 020 7235 3731
Fax: 020 7344 0292
www.bmaa.gv.at/london

Switzerland Tourism
30 Bedford Street
London WC2E 9ED
Tel: 020 7420 4900
e-mail: info.uk@myswitzerland.com
www.uk.myswitzerland.com

The Swiss Embassy
16-18 Montagu Place
London W1H 2BQ
Tel: 020 7616 6000
Fax: 020 7724 7001
www.eda.admin.ch/london

In Germany

The British Embassy
Wilhelmstraße 70-71
10117 Berlin
Tel: 030 20 45 70
e-mail: info@britischebotschaft.de
www.britischebotschaft.de

German Youth Hostel Association (DJH)
Bismarckstraße 8
32756 Detmold
Tel: 05231 7401-0
Fax: 05231 7401-49
e-mail: service@djh.de
www.jugendherberge.de/international

In Austria

The British Embassy
Consular & Visa Section
Jaurèsgasse 10
A-1030 Wien
Tel: 01 71613-5151
Fax: 01 71613-5900
e-mail: visa-consular@britishembassy.at
www.britishembassy.at

Austrian Youth Hostel Association (ÖJHV)
Schottenring 28
A-1010 Wien
Tel: 01 533 5353
Fax: 01 535 0861
e-mail: oejhv-zentrale@oejhv.or.at
www.oejhv.or.at

In Switzerland

The British Embassy
Thunstraße 50
3005 Berne
Tel: 031 359 7700
Fax: 031 359 7701
www.britain-in-switzerland.ch

Swiss Youth Hostels (SJH)
Schaffhauserstraße 14
8042 Zürich
Tel: 01 360 1414
Fax: 01 360 1460
e-mail: bookingoffice@youthhostel.ch
www.youthhostel.ch

Emergency phone numbers in Germany

Police: 110
Fire: 112
Ambulance: 112

Directory enquiries in Germany

There are many different companies offering this service. All numbers
for directory enquiries begin with 118. One of the biggest companies is
Telekom, whose numbers are: 11833 (national) and 11834 (international).
They also offer an English-language service for national numbers: 11837.

CONVERSION TABLES

Note that German uses a comma for the decimal point where English uses a full stop. For example 0.6 would be written 0,6 in German.

Measurements

Only the metric system is used in Germany.

Length
1 cm ≈ 0.4 inches
30 cm ≈ 1 foot

Distance
1 metre ≈ 1 yard
1 km ≈ 0.6 miles

To convert kilometres into miles, divide by 8 and then multiply by 5.

kilometers	1	2	5	10	20	100
miles	0.6	1.25	3.1	6.25	12.50	62.5

To convert miles into kilometres, divide by 5 and then multiply by 8.

miles	1	2	5	10	20	100
kilometers	1.6	3.2	8	16	32	160

Weight
25 g ≈ 1 oz   1 kg ≈ 2 lb   6 kg ≈ 1 stone

To convert kilos into pounds, divide by 5 and then multiply by 11.
To convert pounds into kilos, multiply by 5 and then divide by 11.

kilos	1	2	10	20	60	80
pounds	2.2	4.4	22	44	132	176

Liquid
1 litre ≈ 2 pints
4.5 litres ≈ 1 gallon

Temperature
To convert temperatures in Fahrenheit into Celsius, subtract 32, multiply by 5 and then divide by 9.
To convert temperatures in Celsius into Fahrenheit, divide by 5, multiply by 9 and then add 32.

Fahrenheit (°F)	32	40	50	59	68	86	100
Celsius (°C)	0	4	10	15	20	30	38

Clothes sizes

Sometimes you will find sizes given using the English-language abbreviations **XS** (Extra Small), **S** (Small), **M** (Medium), **L** (Large) and **XL** (Extra Large).

• Women's clothes
Europe	36	38	40	42	44	etc
UK	8	10	12	14	16	

• Bras (cup sizes are the same)
Europe	70	75	80	85	90	etc
UK	32	34	36	38	40	

• Men's shirts (collar size)
Europe	36	38	41	43	etc
UK	14	15	16	17	

• Men's clothes
Europe	40	42	44	46	48	50	etc
UK	30	32	34	36	38	40	

Shoe sizes

• Women's shoes
Europe	37	38	39	40	42	etc
UK	4	5	6	7	8	

• Men's shoes
Europe	40	42	43	44	46	etc
UK	7	8	9	10	11	